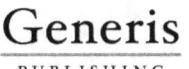

Journey to Different Spiritual Insights

Robby Igusti Chandra

Copyright © 2022 Robby Igusti Chandra
Copyright © 2022 Generis Publishing

All rights reserved. This book or any portion thereof may not be reproduced or used in any manner whatsoever without the written permission of the publisher except for the use of brief quotations in a book review.

Title: Journey to Different Spiritual Insights

ISBN: 979-8-88676-427-7

Author: Robby Igusti Chandra

Cover image: www.pixabay.com

Publisher: Generis Publishing
Online orders: www.generis-publishing.com
Contact email: info@generis-publishing.com

Introduction

Many religious or spiritual teachers use the journey as a figurative language to describe human inner experiences that enable them to sense, embrace, and have a mystical union with the Divine. The universality of few spiritual insights related to such journeys can be seen in particular teachings of the Jewish, Christian, and Islam faith. It also exists in Bahai, Hindu, Buddhist, and many more.

In the past, people who subscribed to such insights might not have wide opportunity to encounter the spiritual paths of others. In the modern age, especially in the digital era where information sharing and networking becomes the basic notion of modern civilization, people can learn different spiritual or religious views that completely offer something different than what they have embraced. They might also encounter various or rich expressions in different religious and spiritual communities that have embedded insights similar to the core of their beliefs. In short, modern civilization can be enriched substantially if those expressions and insights are recognized. Deeper recognition of the uniqueness of one's spirituality or faith can be identified in the middle of many kinds of similar teachings about it. The contrasting differences can also be recognized.

This writing chooses the spiritual journey as a theme to be explored and delved into because the figurative language has become the instrument of communication that fits all kinds of embedded spiritual teaching. The choice is also based on the fact that the spiritual journey has been used surpassing time. In antiquity, such as in Origen's era, or in modern times such as in the indigenous text of Soedjonoredjo, both use the spiritual journey to convey their teaching. The journey also becomes a universal figurative language that surpasses geographic or cultural boundaries as seen in the poems of Yunus Emre, a Turkiye Sufi Master while in the same years, a Franciscan monk does the same in Italy.

The phenomena pose a question for modern people: Why do major world religions recognize and use the spiritual journey allegory or metaphors while simple indigenous spiritual groups in Java, Indonesia also develop such teaching since immemorial time? This writing tries to point to the possibility that the genuine spiritual life should include a willingness to walk in the journey to listen to the voice of other spiritualities, find the differences or contrast, and then appreciate each of them in the process of deepening the recognition and conviction of one's core of spirituality,

This work begins with an exploration of a Javanese poem that contains the narrative of the encounter of Jesus with a Samaritan woman. The poem is a cross-cultural hermeneutic done in the 1920s. The author, Sie Siauw Tjong developed a unique effort to bring the good news to the Javanese indigenous communities by using Islamic and indigenous spiritual terminologies.

The second with the focus on *Homo Viator* is a comparative study between the Parable of the Prodigal Son from the Bible with a Javanese Spiritual Text named *Serat Jatimurti*. The richness of each text is described to expand the readers' awareness of the multiple stages of a spiritual journey.

The last work is a comparison between the spirituality of Yunus Emre and Jacopone da Todi. The focus is on the Divine's love and humans' responses on the same wavelength. Both masters of spirituality are well-known and their legacy is admiringly rich.

Hopefully, in the rapid change in modern societies that have to with many disruptions, a book that ushers the readers toward reflection and awareness of unfinished journey can be contributive.

Jakarta, September 9 2022

An Implicit Good News in a Javanese indigenous religious poem

Abstract

Contextualising biblical teaching entails the adoption of certain forms, terms or thought patterns that might confuse the original message, especially if the effort takes place in a Javanese culture context that is full of subtlety and indirect communication. This study analyses a Javanese poetry form that contains the narrative of Jesus' encounter with a Samaritan woman. The indigenous poems are widely sung by the adherents of Javanese indigenous religions. However, only a few studies are conducted on such indigenous poems that contain Christian messages. This study examines whether or not the poetry form and religious terms that the writer used could serve as a vehicle to convey the good news message of the narrative of John 4:4–42 instead of creating an impediment. Through literary form analysis followed by content analysis, the results showed that the Javanese poem contains several cantos, each with an embedded meaning. Finally, it intends to demonstrate how a combination, instead of contestation, of the indigenous, Islam and Christian terms is effective for the writer's purpose. Thus, the writer's choice was suitable in his effort to communicate the original teaching.

This study contributes to inter-religious communication by identifying the Javanese indigenous communication pattern, particularly the placement of their messages inside their poem's structure and in various terminologies. Strengthening inter-religious communication to create a mutual understanding in Indonesian pluralistic society is needed especially as the Javanese indigenous religions are often misunderstood.

Keywords: indigenous poem; inter-religious communication; indirect communication; Javanese; spiritual teaching; narrative.

Introduction

The Javanese indigenous religions use various forms of arts, such as literature, music or dance, to communicate their philosophy, spiritual teachings or ethics. One of them is suluk. In its essence, suluk is a spiritual teaching that takes the form of poetry. According to Prabowo (2015:1), the word suluk in the Javanese literary tradition is used for writings containing a mystical mixture of Islamic teachings and Javanese indigenous spiritual views. Similarly, in his study, Akbar points out that suluk is a journey to gain God's acceptance by emptying one's self from uncleanliness and filling it with what Allah wants (Akbar 2006:82). Thus, the essence of suluk is teaching about the mystical journey and human existence.

When conveying their suluk, spiritual leaders also voice or sing it. Hastanto (1983) mentions that the Javanese call such spiritual teaching poems that they sing tembang and Suwardi (2015:19) calls them tembang macapat. Tembang macapat has a set of strict rules related to the number of syllables, lines, melody or cantos to be voiced to create the intended atmosphere for the audience. Macapat is multi-functional as it can serve as the bearer of a message, narrative, teaching or as a medium to convey ambiguity, puzzles and others (Purna, Astuti & Wahyuningsih 1996:3). Darsono states that for their spiritual ceremonies, the Javanese have developed hundreds of tembang macapat since around the year 1500 (Darsono 2016:30). In short, tembang macapat is an indirect communication method that offers the audience a space to reflect on the meaning of reality or their lives.

Concerning indirect communication, Sukarno (2010) mentions that the Javanese people more significantly observe some concepts that are well rooted in their culture; among those concepts is the concept of *tanggap sasmita* or being able to catch the hidden meaning. Most audiences in the Javanese culture are expected to be able to discover the real meaning of the message, although it might be multi-interpretable. Kierkegaard mentions that such inwardness cannot be communicated directly because expressing it directly makes it orientate outwardly, not inwardly (Kierkegaard 1992:260). Inwardness means that in the process of interpreting an embedded message, it is often suggested that the audience delve inwardly into their existing insights. Oppositely, in much direct communication, when everything is expressed more explicitly there is no need for the audience to actively find its meaning, as the meaning is clear and not multi-interpretable.

In his study, Turnbull (2008:15) mentions that a Javanese indigenous religious poem, one of their indirect communication methods to convey the message of Jesus' encounter with the Samaritan woman, might cause impediment, multi-interpretation or ambiguity as the poem has an embedded message in its structure or flow. Yet according to Nagamoto (2000), the Javanese seem to live with 'the logic of not'. The finding of Nagamoto concerning 'the logic of not' echoes the cultural dimension concept. It means the Javanese, including the adherents of their indigenous religion, live in a high-context culture instead of a social relationship where everything is spelt out explicitly (Hofstede 2011).

In 1923, Sie Siauw Tjong wrote Serat Suluk Pawestri Samariyah (hereafter referred to as Suluk Samariyah). The title means The Spiritual Text for a Samaritan Woman. Prabowo (2015:34), who first researched the Biblical message in Suluk Samariyah, states that this poem is a tembang macapat. He mainly analyses the term 'living water', and then finds that the message is similar to the original one. The Javanese who use suluk mostly belong to a belief or religion that in Indonesia today is known as *Penghayat Kepercayaan*. The term penghayat means 'practitioners' and *Kepercayaan* means 'faith or belief' (Muttaqin 2012:29). *Penghayat Kepercayaan* (hereinafter referred to as *penghayat*) are the followers or practitioners of an amalgamated group of indigenous spiritualities. In Indonesia today, the term penghayat can also mean the indigenous religion. The effort of Sie Siauw Tjong to produce indigenous literature in the form of a Javanese poem shows his appreciation for Javanese culture and beliefs because, as Hastanto states, the Javanese poems have strict rules concerning their structure, syllables, the number of sentences and melodies (Hastanto 1983:120).

The focus of this study is to uncover the author's method in using the Javanese indigenous poetry forms, including the modification of its features, as the embedded Javanese indigenous religious teachings in them can obscure the original message of good news about Divine love and grace from John 4:4–42. It also explores whether the writer's use of various religious vocabularies or terms in the content of the poem obscures the original meaning. The findings are expected to enrich inter-religious communication methods mainly by adopting a certain literary form as an indirect communication method or to convey implicit messages.

Methodology

This study is descriptive qualitative research, with Suluk Samariyah and John 4:4–42 as its sources. Four publications concerning Suluk Samariyah serve as the source. Firstly, the original book in Javanese script was written by Sie Siauw Tjong in 1923 (Sie 1923). Secondly, the Javanese language edition is written in the Latin alphabet that the writer published in 1925 (Sie 1925). Two published translations of the suluk into Indonesian were also used. The first translation is the work of Prabowo (2015) contained in his research, although it consists of only the main part of Suluk Samariyah, and the other translation is done by Sunyoto in 2021, which is the whole text in Indonesian (Sie 2021).

Firstly, using the literary form or poetry analysis, the study collects data about the narratives in the cantos contained in *Suluk Samariyah*. Secondly, the study also checks data concerning the sequence of the cantos in the poem. Thirdly, the study lists the differences in the message of the narratives in Suluk Samariyah with John 4: 4–42 by also focusing on the writer's choice of the terminologies that derive from Javanese indigenous religions or others to describe the identity of Jesus. After the above steps, the study analyses the implicit and explicit messages that might exist in the suluk and performs a textual interpretation of their combined meaning. The focus is to analyse the implicit messages in the combination of the cantos and their sequence; then an analysis is also done on the explicit message in the usage of terminologies that derive from Islam or Javanese indigenous culture and spirituality.

At last, the combined meaning of the implicit and explicit messages are explored. Based on the results of the analyses, the study presents the conclusion concerning the consequences of the adoption or modification of the indigenous forms of communication and terminologies, with the risk of deviation from the original message of the good news.

Results and discussion

Background

The *Penghayat* live on various islands; however, the largest numbers of them live in Java, and most Indonesians might interchangeably name those who live in Central and East Java as the followers of *Kebathinan* [inner life], *Kawruh sanyutaan* [knowledge of the truth), *Kejawen* [Javanese spirituality] or *agama Jawa* [Javanese religion] (Muttaqin 2012:26). The term *agama Jawa* (Javanese religion) originates from the book of Clifford Geertz (1976). Many Indonesians still view the indigenous religions as syncretic, superstitious, pantheistic or monistic and their indigenous literature as illogical and mystical (Hamudy & Rifki 2020:51). The study of Zoetmulder (1991) explores whether the Javanese indigenous religions are more pantheistic or monistic, a classification that does not come from the framework of their own beliefs. Their believers still retain their spirituality, beliefs and ethics in their communities. A study conducted by Arafah et al. (in Samsurijjal et al. 2019:954) in the Lombok area shows that they convey their philosophy, spiritual views and teachings indirectly by using poems that they chant.

Since the 17th century, Islamic leaders have developed various creative contextualizations (Hidayatullah 2019:102). Fathurahman (2017) proves that their success is significant. Ricklefs (2006) also shows that many Islamic leaders embed their teachings in traditional rituals or indigenous poetry forms. Mulyono (2012) shows that Islamic views influence the form and values contained in traditional Javanese literature including macapat. In comparison, only a few Christian leaders make the effort to bridge the cultural and spiritual gaps between them and the indigenous religions, even today.

Suluk Samariyah was written by Sie Siauw Tjong in 1923. He is of Chinese descent and a member of a Gerevormeerde Kerk (a reformed church) that Nederland Zending Vereniging [the Netherland mission fellowship] started near his hometown. As a businessman, he is conversant with Dutch, Javanese, everyday Mandarin and Malay languages. The work might indicate that he is a real pioneer in creating inter-religious appreciation, especially between *Christians* and *Penghayat*.

Analysing the literary form of Suluk Samariyah

The published translation of Suluk Samariyah in Indonesian consists of six major parts or cantos. Subsequently, there are 16, 18, 19, 33, 14 and 22 stanzas in those cantos. The first stanza in the opening canto is as follows:

> *wuryaning kang sinarkarèng tulis*
> *tèsing sêdya syaga malat prana*
> *nênangi conging tujune*
> *juwêt ngrawit mrih jumbuh*
> *danurwedha wêwarah jati*
> *dêdamar kauripan*
> *mãngga dipun gayuh*
> *saiyêg saeka praya*
> *yèn wus nyandhak ywa sinimpên tan wèh mijil*
> *nging sami dèn wradinna (Sie 2021:14)*

> [Apparent the meaning of writing,
> contained in the words,
> to calm down the heart is the goal,
> because it is an attractive wish that fits,
> with the knowledge of the sacred teaching
> that illumines life,
> go reach with the spirit of one word, one intention,
> when it is obtained,
> should not be saved,
> but to be shared with our fellows].

After the first stanza, the canto describes the journey of Jesus:

> *Kawuwusa wau kangjeng nabi*
> *Arsa kundur mring tanah dunungnya*
> *Galileyah doh parane*
> *Lampahira karuhun*
> *Anglangkungi tanah kekalih*
> *Preyah Samariyah*
> *Nging satunggilipun*
> *Yeku kang aran Pereyah*

> *Yen medala ing ngriku saklangkung tebih*
> *Nging dadya padatannya (Sie 2021:17)*

> [It is narrated that the Lord Prophet
> will return to his homeland
> Galilea which is far
> The normal journey
> will pass through two regions
> that is called Samaritan
> and the other one is Parea
> passing through those regions makes the journey farther
> but it has been customary].

Furthermore, the first canto describes the well and the relationship between the Jews and the Samaritans, as well as Jesus' decision to stop by the well. In the end, there is an explanation that the encounter of Jesus with the Samaritan woman has been God's intention. In the second canto, the writer describes Jesus' request for water and the woman's response. She begins by speaking to herself about Jesus' initiative to speak to her. She then questions Jesus. The narration continues with Jesus' word concerning the living water; the woman questions Jesus about his words for her, but he does not have any pail to get any water. She even speaks about Jacob.

In the third canto, Jesus shows his understanding of the woman's questions. The canto begins as follows:

> *Nabi Ngisa ngandika rus*
> *Nini away wancak driya*
> *Sun warah tilingna age*
> *Banyune sumur punika,*
> *Sing sapa anginuma,*
> *Maksih ngelak akiripun,*
> *Analyane punang toya (Sie 2021:39)*

> [Gently the Prophet Jesus speaks,
> O lady, do not be bothered,
> Let me inform you,

See the well next to you,
the water of the well,
Whoever drinks from it,
Will be thirsty again in the end,
there is another water]

This canto is ended with the description of how the woman feels sad and remembers her past after Jesus mentions that she has lived with five husbands and that the man who lives with her now is not her husband. Then, the canto places the last line in the last stanza '*Lir mendhung ngumpul nglimputi, ilang kabuncang maruta*' [like a dark cloud gathers to cover, disappears blown by the wind'] (Sie 2021:48).

The fourth canto consists of the continuation of Jesus' words for the woman, mainly about the true worshipper who worships in Spirit and Truth. There are few explanations about its meaning and the description of the woman's response. The last two stanzas depict the woman's happiness for the encounter and Jesus' declaration that he is the one that the woman has been waiting for.

Dhuh babo sang awiku
Cecengkluken gyan ulun mangayun
Majanmane utusanira Hyang Widhi
Upami lamun wus rawuh
Wewarah in karahayon

Sang Ngisa ngandika rum
Amalehken ig kaananipun
Adhuh babo kalingane sira nini
Wreuhanta kang sira ruruh
'Ya ingsun ingkang kawiyos' (Sie 2021:63)

['O Teacher,
in each of my steps, I look to find
the representative of the Almighty
when he comes
will teach about salvation'

Jesus speaks to change the condition
'O, Lady, remember

and know that who you see
Yes, I have already come']

The next canto describes Jesus' disciples who rejoin him after buying food in a nearby place and their responses. This canto also emphasises the woman's impact on her village as she speaks about Jesus. The last canto is the closing of the narrative with the teaching given by Jesus to the disciples. The writer also adds a comment that the happiness of Jesus is like a farmer who sees the growth and harvest of what he or she has planted. Then, the last line of *Suluk Samariyah* describes Jesus' return journey home.

According to Prabowo (2015:34), *Suluk Samariyah* is a teaching of how to live in perfection after God gives living water or salvation to a human being. *Suluk Samariyah* in the Javanese traditional alphabet was published in 1923 in Gemblegan, Solo, Central Java (see Sie 1923) and then in 1925 in Bandung (see Sie 1925). Prabowo, from the Language Institute of Yogyakarta, Indonesia, translated the main part of the work in 2015. The complete text in the Javanese Latin alphabet with Indonesian translation appeared in 2021 as the work of Sunyoto (see Sie 2021). Those translations do not have significant differences.

In John 4:4–42, the author depicts Jesus as a weary person who decides to take a rest near a well. As he rests, a Samaritan woman comes to the well. According to the narrative in John 4, Jesus straightforwardly requests water from the woman. In comparison, the first stanza of the second canto of *Suluk Samariyah* describes Jesus observing the woman before speaking to her with the lengthy wording 'do be careful when you draw the water, can you give me a bit to quench my thirst' (Sie 2021:11). Jesus appears as a gentle person.

This *suluk* takes the form of *tembang macapat,* which means that it is a poem to be sung or voiced and consists of many *cantos* (major divisions of a poem). Santosa demonstrates that *macapat* is multi-functional, to be used for a traditional aesthetical ceremony that contains spiritual guidance and a traditional incantation (Santosa 2016:89–92). As a method of teaching, a religious teacher often combines *tembang macapat* with a shadow puppet show (*wayang*) and *gamelan* (a traditional musical instrument) to surround the audience with an atmosphere intended for deep spiritual reflection.

Suluk Samariyah is to be sung as *tembang macapat*. It consists of 11 cantos and each has its unique poetry metrum (Saddhono & Pramestuti 2018:16). The names are *Maskumambang* [a foetus in the womb], *Mijil* [birth], *Sinom* [growing], *Kinanthi* [educating], *Asmaradana* [love and romance], *Dhandhanggula* [adulthood and sweet expectation], *Pangkur* [principles], *Durma* [sharing], *Gambuh* [connecting and uniting], *Megatruh* [separation of body and spirit] and *Pocung* [death]. The most authoritative researcher in this field, Padmosoekotjo, posits in his study that there are nine cantos in *tembang macapat*. He states that there is one Kawi song (namely Girisa) and five *macapat tengah* (namely *Gambuh, Mêgatruh or Dudukwuluh, Balabak, Wirangrong and Jurudêmung*) which are often combined with *Macapat* songs although they belong to a different category of poems (Padmosoekotjo 1953). When listening to a canto, its audience is thereby given a clue about its embedded message or the spiritual teaching to be reflected upon (Padmosoekotjo 1960).

The different views concerning the number of cantos in *tembang macapat* are understandable because, based on the language and structure, *tembang macapat* can be categorized as *tembang gedhe* or 'great poem' with its high-level language or *tembang cilik* and *tengahan (small and middle)*, which use the simpler Javanese language but are different in length (Padmosoekotjo 1960).

As shown in some *suluk* such as *Suluk Wujil* (Fanani 2018) or *Serat Suluk Padmoroso* (Fanani 2018), they only consist of several cantos to emphasise the message that they teach. Thus, not the whole cantos that depict the total sequences of life are included in some *suluk*. Each name and set of characteristics indicates its embedded message.

The writer of *Suluk Samariyah* constructs his *macapat* by choosing only six *cantos* instead of the whole 11. As they appear in order, they are *Dhandhanggula* [adulthood or sweet expectation], *Sinom* [growing and struggling], *Asmarandana* [love], *Gambuh* [harmonizing and uniting], *Mijil* [birth], and *Kinanthi* [educating]. In short, the six cantos describe only parts or stages of the whole life cycle. He begins with *Dhandhanggula*, which means expectation for good things as adults. His message and reason can be described as follows:

1. In reciting *Suluk Samariyah*, one finds the *Dhandhanggula macapat* in the beginning. Conventionally, this poetry division conveys an adult dream or expectation for goodness to come. The word *Dhandhanggula* means expectation, yearning and fantasy of a person in the adult stage of life, while *Gula* means 'sweet' (Noviati 2018:51). The writer places this *Dhandhanggula* instead of *Maskumamba*ng or *Mijil*, as the beginning of the whole narrative of the *Suluk Samariyah* might signify that he intends to

use the poem to make the audience reflect on sweet dreams or expectations in life instead of focusing on the meaning of human birth. Although the narrative in *Dhandhanggula* is the same as the original one at the beginning of John 4:4–42, it conveys a different atmosphere or tone. The original tone is related to Jesus' intention to pause after his long journey. By using *Dhandhanggula*, the author gives us clue that the audience is led to reflect on a good dream or longing to be fulfilled. In stanza 15, the author explicitly writes, '*pambukanya kang kinăntha ring hyang, mangkana pan wus pasthine, dhawahirèng kang wahyu, nugrahane punang pawèstri*' which means 'from the beginning of the Almighty has ascertained, revelation will come down for the woman' (Sie 2021). Thus, the good dream belongs to the Almighty, who has planned that the woman would receive Divine grace, later to be liberated from a curse and cleansed from bondage. In short, at the beginning of *Suluk Samariyah,* there is a direct and indirect message that the whole teaching of this *suluk* is about God's sweet dream, expectation or intention to give grace to beloved humans or about humans' sweet expectation of their lives when they encounter Jesus.

2. Directly after the *Dhandhanggula*, there is *Sinom*. The number of lines, the stanza and the vowels at the end of each sentence of *Sinom* differ from *Dhandhanggula*, and the audience recognises the clue that it describes the growing stage of youth (Saddhono & Pramestuti 2018). *Sinom* teaches about a journey to find the real self while struggling with curiosity and emotional issues. The placement of *Sinom* directly after *Dhandhanggula* might indicate the author's embedded message that after humans have a dream, there are struggles. In its narrative, Jesus takes the initiative to start a dialogue with the Samaritan woman, an act that intrigues the woman, as shown in the last part of *Dhandhanggula* and the first part of *Sinom*. The last stanza of *Dhandhanggula* is as follows:

Nabi Ngisa tan samar pangèksi
mring pawèstri kang tigas kawuryan
kadadyanira ing têmbe
sinawang calon punjul
bisa tampi wasitèng gaib
wus pinasthi dening Hyang
rahayu tinêmu
ing dunya praptèng ngakerat

> *kangjêng nabi arsa ngruwat mring pawèstri*
> *tarunaning tyasira (Sie 2021:24)*

> [The Prophet Jesus does not hesitate
> to watch the innocent woman
> who in the future
> will become significant
> in receiving revelation
> that God determines
> salvation everlasting
> as the Prophet Jesus will restore the woman
> youthful life.]

The *Sinom* stanza is as follows:

> *Nabi Ngisa lon ngandika*
> *hèh nini mara dèn aglis*
> *nimba aywa ringa-ringa*
> *sun jaluk banyu sathithik (Sie 2021:25)*

> [The Prophet Jesus says
> O young lady,
> do draw the water carefully
> give me a bit]

The author follows the original script in the Gospel which describes Jesus' request for water from the woman, but the woman responds differently. She does not directly reply but speaks to herself. There are words such as 'surprised' and 'questions' explicitly placed in this canto that strengthen the implicit message of the *Sinom* canto. As *Sinom* indicates struggle or, more precisely, inner struggles, this canto might describe the struggle of the woman in her youthfulness and her life.

Thus far, the narratives in the first two cantos are the same as the original narrative:

1. The third canto is *Asmarandana*. By listening to the vowels and number of lines, the audience recognises that it is a longing, love, care and intimacy canto. According to Mulyono, the audience knows that they are led to reflect inwardly on the meaning of love, longing, care and intimacy by being immersed in the atmosphere created by the sound, melody, music and rhythm (Mulyono

2012:107). The content shows the characteristics of the Samaritan woman, who has a perceptive mind besides being reflective. She also keeps her feelings inside. In short, although the narrative is the same as the original one, the author depicts the Samaritan woman in the *poetry* as a Javanese woman who has been walking on the wrong path of life. Thus, in *Asmarandana*, indirect teaching is communicated: to achieve one's dream, a struggling phase takes place. Only by filling one's heart with God's love can life become meaningful. God through Jesus gently offers it as an unconditional gift or good news

2. The following canto is *Gambuh*, which communicates a harmony or agreement concerning the steps to be taken in life. Connected with the *Asmarandana*, *Gambuh* depicts harmony or even intimacy between two persons. To be able to receive such an opportunity as a grace, *Gambuh* stanza 14 explicitly introduces a concept of God as *rama amêngku wiraos* or 'Father who controls the human heart' (Sie 2021). The concept of God as a father is alien to most of the Javanese indigenous religions, as they view God as abstract and beyond human words to explain. In *Gambuh* stanzas 15 and 16, the writer inserts explicit teaching about a loving God who relates to humans like a father. This concept is compared with the Samaritan image of God (Sie 2021). Undeniably, *Gambuh* stanzas 15 and 16 explicitly introduce the audience to a concept of God from the original teaching of John 4:4–42. Furthermore, *Gambuh* stanza 30 points out that the Samaritan woman has a turning point experience as her dream to encounter the messenger of the Almighty and God's love is fulfilled.

3. The following part of *Suluk Samariyah* is *Mijil*. It consists of a reflection on birth. Purposely, the author does not place *Mijil* as the beginning of *Suluk Samariyah*, an unusual order that his audience recognises. Implicitly, the writer uses it to convey that when the woman receives God's grace, she experiences a new life or a turning point in life.

4. Finally, *Kinanthi* closes *Suluk Samariyah*. The word *Kinanthi* comes from the word *kanthi*, which means 'holding hands.' The poem indicates a flavour of joyfulness. It depicts two persons who have encountered each other deciding to continue their life journey by doing it together. In *Kinanthi*, the author explicitly explains the message of his poem, something that the original narratives in John 4 do not have.

Through the analysis of the characteristics of each canto of *Suluk Samariyah*, this study finds that the teaching is communicated implicitly. The author draws his audience to reflect on the meaning of their lives, which consists of a dream, struggles, mistakes, needs for reconciliation, turning points and commitment to a meaningful life. The unique message in *Suluk Samariyah* centres on a loving God who gives grace and new life to humans.

The writer placed implicitly the central teaching of John 4:4–42 about God's unconditional love and grace in *Asmaradana* canto. The canto is his effort to signify the encounter of Jesus and the woman as the encounter between a human being and a loving heavenly figure who cares for that human being. The loving, gentle and caring character of Jesus is explicitly described therein. As the woman does not easily accept the grace, later the author uses *Gambuh* to elaborate the teaching explicitly. In *Mijil,* the writer also communicates that each person could experience a new spiritual birth or a turning point when receiving God's love. Thus, the poem teaches that in the human journey, there is a point when God offers love and intimacy as grace for them or the good news. The analysis shows that Sie Siauw Tjong manages to use the forms of cantos with their embedded meaning that the audience is familiar with to convey the good news about God's love and grace.

Analysing the usage of the indigenous religious vocabulary or terminology

Concerning many terms that the author places in the poems, there are two kinds of terminologies. The first kind originates from the Javanese indigenous religions and the second comes from either Islamic or Christian vocabularies.

Ruwatan

In *Dhandhanggula*, stanzas 12–15, there is the following sentence: '*kanjeng nabi arsa ngruwat mring pawestri*' [the Lord Prophet intends to clean the woman] (Sie 2021). In indigenous spirituality, *ngruwat* (verb) or *ruwatan* (noun) can be translated as an act to cleanse dirt and disruption to free human beings. According to Rukiyah, the term is similar to 'recovering', 'balancing', 'healing' or 'harmonising' (Rukiyah 2017:5). Kristriyanto states that *ruwatan* can also be understood as expressed by this sentence: *ruwatan minangka tumindaking manungsa kangge pados kawilujengan* [*ruwatan* is the human act in seeking salvation or freedom from disaster] (Kristriyanto 2018:42–43). To be free as such, humans need to take the initiative, especially in finding a divine figure to help.

Thus with the term *ngruwat* in *Suluk Samariyah*, the author portrays a woman who needs to find someone who can help her obtain recovery or reconciliation, similarly to John 4:4–42.

In the last three lines of this canto, the writer inserts terms such as 'salvation', 'forgiveness' and 'life' as three dimensions of grace, something that in John 4:4–42 does not exist. The addition of such a line might signify the author's effort to merge the biblical concept of unconditional grace, love and God's initiative that is foreign to the audience with the idea of *ruwatan* that they are familiar with.

Two-in-one, Jurubasuki, Plawanganira and *Rohullah wa kalimatuhu*

In *Asmarandana* stanza 7, the author writes *Nabi Ngisa wrangkanèki dadya loroning atunggal*, which means, 'Jesus the Prophet blends to become *two-in-one*' (Sie 2021). The term *two-in-one* does not derive from the Javanese indigenous or Islamic culture. In the indigenous beliefs and Christian faith context, the adherents might interpret such a term to mean that Jesus is the manifestation of a divine-human union. Zoetmulder (1991) finds in his study that the Javanese indigenous religions teach a concept of *Manunggaling Kawula Gusti* or divine-human union. Thus, the usage of the term *two-in-one* can help the audience who are familiar with such a concept to understand that Jesus' essence is not the same as that of all humans, but a union of God's and human essence in one person.

In Gambuh stanza 28, when the writer summarises the teaching of Jesus to the woman, three more terms appear: *Juru basuki* [peacemaker], *plawanganira Hyang Agung* [door to God] and *Jêng Ngisa Rohullah* [Jesus, the Spirit of God] (Sie 2021). The concept of the peacemaker is common in many cultures. The term *Ngisa Rohullah* needs to be analysed carefully. Ibn Manẓūr states that the word *ruh* or spirit comes from the word *al rih* or in plural *kalimah*, which means 'wind' or 'breath'. Breath means the human activity of inhalation and exhalation. Also, as humans cannot live without breath, *ruh* means life. Thus, *Ngisa Rohullah* means that Jesus originated from the Spirit of God and can give life (Ibn Manẓūr 2011:356).

Mahmoud Ayoub, an Islamic scholar from America, explains that Jesus Christ was a special case among the prophets; he did 'not receive the revelation or the word of God as a divine communication, but he was the very 'word of God sent to Mary. According to him, the term *kalimah* concerning God has three aspects: decree or ordinance (Q. 10:33), source of blessing or judgement (Q. 7:137) and revelation (Q. 2:37, 2:124) (Ayoub 1986:70).

More fundamentally, the Qur'ān relates the term 'Spirit of God' not exclusively to Jesus. The Spirit of God breathed into Adam so that the first human could live (Q. 15:29). The birth of Jesus also happened by such an inspiration of God, as one verse says. Thus in Islam, Jesus is not the incarnation of God (Harmakaputra 2013:92).

Two scholars, Badhurulhisham and Hambali (2018) state in their study that the word *Rohullah* indicates that the essence of Jesus as God's creation is beyond human understanding, based on the Qur'ān verse in Surah al-Nisa 4:171–172: [*T*]ruly, the Messiah Jesus of Mary is only God's ambassador and God's word that God has conveyed to Mary, and he is also the breath of the Spirit that derived from God. (p. 88)

Theologically, McGrath (2001) states that the concept of the Spirit of God in the term *Rohullah wa kalimatuhu* in Islam might be similar to the Christology of the Gospel of John, as it never portrays Jesus as identical to God, but rather as God's legitimate (and only) agent. However, two scholars differ from him: Koester (2003:83) states that the author of the Gospel of John conveys Jesus to the readers by using familiar categories only to make them realise later that Jesus cannot be limited to any one of them; similarly, Van der Merwe (2019) states that in the Gospel of John, the author presents Jesus as a 'puzzle'. Undoubtedly, he is human, yet he is one with God. He is a rabbi and a healer who provides life by dying. However, in the end, Merwe concludes that 'the Gospel of John's uniqueness in early Christian literature entails its special patterns of language to describe Jesus who is the Christ, the Son of God' (Van der Merwe 2019:1).

However, concerning the message of John 4:4–42 in the text, Jesus affirms that he is the Messiah; thus no difference appears with the meaning of *nabi Ngisa Rohullah* in Islam. A Muslim audience might hold the concept that Jesus is simply a superior prophet or divine messenger. Indigenous religious believers might conclude that Jesus is a mysterious Spirit of God or even the divine incarnation. Javanese Christians can accept such a message from John 4, but only by connecting it to the whole message concerning the Divinity of Christ in the Gospel of John. Therefore, the writer of *Suluk Samariyah* communicates the message by using a term that can become multi-interpretable.

There is also a description of Jesus as *plawanganira* or the Door. Such a term is echoed in John 10:9, which teaches that Jesus does not play the role only as an entrance in John 10, but also his function as a loving God is to keep the sheep inside after they enter.

It can be summarized that the writer uses terminologies that can be classified as belonging to the Javanese indigenous religions, Christian concepts and Islam. For those who only pay attention to the combination of them, the meaning can be obscure. However, the Javanese indigenous religion adherents might view it differently as they relate the terminologies with the forms or cantos and their embedded meaning as has been described above.

Discussion

The Javanese *Penghayat* adherents in particular often use implicit messages in their communication. Their habit to use indirect communication and hidden messages frequently might contribute to many misunderstandings in Indonesian society about their belief. People view them as obscure, superstitious or animistic and pantheistic. Even the modern Indonesian government has only shown them equal treatment to other believers since 2017.

Sie Siauw Tjong's choice to combine the usage of *tembang macapat* as a literary form does not create an impediment or obscurity for the audience. In his studies about one of the Asian poems, Franke (2016) states that it is customary for them, particularly in China, to use implicit or indirect messages and even nothingness in a poetic form to make sense. Bowe et al. (2012) state that they are accustomed to grasping hidden or implicit meanings in the characteristics of each canto where the narrative is placed or in the terminologies.

There is no explicit description of Jesus as the Son of God, but indirectly, using the terms 'the Peacemaker', *Rohullah* or 'the Door', added with Christian terms related to God such as 'grace', 'salvation', 'love' and the Javanese terms 'two-in-one' and *ngruwat*, implicitly the poem gives hints that Jesus is God's spirit who loves human beings. Indirectly, the writer gives space for the audience to reflect that either Jesus is a divine incarnation where God and his humanity unite, or he is neither divine nor human. Jesus becomes a complex puzzle, which mirrors the view of the indigenous religion's adherents, which holds that God's reality is too complicated to be expressed anthropomorphically.

Hofstede's concept of cultural dimensions as discussed by Sari (Sari 2021:39) might support the statement and signify the value of the writer's usage of multi-interpretable or ambiguous vocabularies or terminologies. As the Javanese culture is often classified as a high-context culture, such ambiguity enables the audience to connect each poetry element with the cantos, terminology, sound, atmosphere or the narrative in the communication process. Speakers who use such an indirect method to convey the message are valued as giving space for the audience to take part in revealing its meaning. The writer creates such a method as he is also aware that his Javanese audience lives with what Cox-Joseph names the neither-nor or both-as-well-as logic (Cox-Joseph 2020), which can help them recognise the good news message in the teaching of *Suluk Samariyah,* which is the original message of John 4: 4–42.

Conclusion

Indigenous religious poetry as the form that communicates the message of John 4:4–42 indirectly fits with the Javanese Penghayat adherent's custom. This finding is significant as most studies about their poems primarily focus on their contents or vocabularies instead of the structure or form.

By using many Javanese indigenous religious terminologies besides the Christian or Islamic ones, the writer opens a space for his audience to reflect on the whole message of Suluk Samariyah, which is about the good news that God in Jesus grants unconditional love, an idea that the writer explicitly elaborates several times. Such a method of giving the audience space to recognise the hidden message fits their culture and might cause positive responses.

The result of this study hints that indirect methods of communication might fit in a communication process within the penghayat context rather than direct messages. As the study is based more on literature, an empirical survey might be needed to prove its findings.

References

Akbar, M.A., 2006, 'Studi Tentang Suluk Dalam Tarekat Naqsyabandiyah Khalidiyah Aminiyah (Study on Suluk in Naqsyabandiyah Khalidiyah Aminiyah Community)', PhD thesis, Universitas Islam Negeri Yogyakarta.

Ayoub, M., 1986, 'The word of God in Islam', in E. Vaporis (ed.), Orthodox Christians and Muslims, pp. 69–78, Holy Cross Orthodox Press, Brookline, MA.

Badhrulhisham, A. & Hambali, K.M.K., 2018, 'Konsep Roh Suci Menurut Islam dan Kristian (The concept of Holy Spirit in Islam and Christianity)', Jurnal Akidah & Pemikiran Islam 20(1), 85–108.

Bowe, H., Martin, K., Bowe, H. & Martin, K., 2012, 'Direct and indirect messages: The role of social context identified by Grice and Searle', Communication Across Cultures, pp. 9–25, Cambridge University Press, Cambridge, UK.

Cox-Joseph, T., 2020, 'Hidden meanings', Chest 142(4), 1069. https://doi.org/10.1378/ chest.11-2849

Darsono, 2016, 'Beberapa Pandangan Tentang Tembang Macapat (several views about Tembang Macapat)', Keteg: Jurnal Pemikiran, Pengetahuan, dan Kajian Tentang Bunyi 16(1), 27–38.

Fanani, A., 2018, 'The Javanese quest of Islamic spirituality in Suluk Wujil: A Semiotic reading', Analisa: Journal of Social Science and Religion 3(02), 221–238. DOI https:// doi.org/10.18784/analisa.v3i02.654

Fathurahman, O., 2017, 'Sejarah Pengkafiran dan Marginalisasi Paham Keagamaan di Melayu dan Jawa: Sebuah Telaah Sumber (The history of blamimg and marginalization of religious doctrine in Malay and Java: An analysis on sources)', Analisis: Jurnal Studi Keislaman 11(2), 447–474.

Franke, W., 2016, 'Nothingness and the aspiration to universality in the poetic "making" of sense: An essay in comparative east-west poetics', Asian Philosophy 26(3), 241–264.

Geertz, C., 1976, Religion of Java, rev. ed., University of Chicago Press, Chicago, IL.

Hamudy, M.I.A. & Rifki, M.S., 2020, 'Civil rights of the believers of unofficial religions (Penghayat Kepercayaan) in Pekalongan District', Jurnal Antropologi: Isu-Isu Sosial Budaya 22(1), 48–58.

Harmakaputra, H.A., 2013, 'A preliminary research on the Islamic concept of Jesus as the Spirit and word of God: From polemics towards a comparative theology', Jurnal Teologi Indonesia 1(1), 90–102. https://doi.org/10.46567/ijt.v1i1.93

Hastanto, S., 1983, 'Tembang Macapat in Central Java', Proceedings of the Royal Musical Association 110, 118–127. https://doi.org/10.1093/jrma/110.1.118

Hidayatullah, A., 2019, 'Paradigma Dakwah Kultural: Dimensi Sufisme dalam Kontruksi Karakter Bima pada Pewayangan Jawa (Paradigm of Cultural Daqwah: Sufistic Dimension in the Contruct of Bima Character in Javanese

Shadow Puppet)', *Jurnal Ilmu Dakwah* 39(2), 101. https://doi.org/10.21580/jid.v39.2.4409

Hofstede, G., 2011, 'Dimensionalizing cultures: The Hofstede Model in context', *Online Readings in Psychology and Culture* 2(1), 1–26. https://doi.org/10.9707/2307- 0919.1014

Ibn Manẓūr, M. ibn M., 2011, *Lisān al-'Arab*, 3rd edn., Dār, Ṣādir, Beirut.

Kierkegaard, S., 1992, *Concluding unscientific postscript to philosophical fragments*, Princeton University Press, Princeton, NJ.

Kristriyanto, 2018, 'Yesus Kristus Juru Ruwat Manusia: Sebuah Pendekatan Semiotika dalam Gereja Kristen Jawa (Jesus Christ, the liberator of human life: A semiotic approach in the Javanese Christian Church)', *Kurios* 4(1), 39–56. https://doi. org/10.30995/kur.v4i1.32

Koester, C.R., 2003, *Symbolism in the Fourth Gospel: meaning, mystery, community*, Fortress Press, Minneapolis, MN.

McGrath, J.F., 2001, *John's Apologetic Christology: Legitimation And Development In Johannine Christology*, Cambridge University Press, Cambridge, MA.

Mulyono, A.S., 2012, 'Pengaruh Islam terhadap Perkembangan Budaya Jawa: Tembang Macapat', *El Harakah* 14(1), 115–136. https://doi.org/10.18860/el.v0i0.2196

Muttaqin, A., 2012, 'Islam and the changing meaning of spirituality in contemporary Indonesia', *Al-Jami'ah: Journal of Islamic Studies* 50(1), 23–56. https://doi.org/10.14421/ajis.2012.501.23-56

Nagatomo, S., 2000, 'The logic of the diamond Sutra: A is not A, therefore it is A', *Asian Philosophy* 10(3), 213–244. https://doi.org/10.1080/09552360020011277

Noviati, E., 2018, 'Eksistensi nilai-nilai Tembang Macapat di kalangan anak muda sebagai filter pengaruh alkuturasi (Existence of Tembang Macapat Values among the young generation as filter of acculturation influence)', *Dewa Ruci: Jurnal Pengkajian dan Penciptaan Seni* 13(1), 49–62. https://doi.org/10.33153/dewaruci. v13i1.2505

Padmosoekotjo, S., 1953, *Ngengrengan Kasusastraan Djawa, Jilid II (Frowing at the Javanese Literature, book II)*, Penerbit & Toko Buku Hien Hoo Sing, Yogyakarta.

Padmosoekotjo, S., 1960, *Ngengrengan Kasusastran Djawa I, II (Frowning at the Javanese Literature Book 1 & 2)*, Penerbit & Toko Buku Hien Hoo Sing, Yogyakarta.

Prabowo, 2015, 'Serat Suluk Pawestri Samariyah: Sebuah Pencarian Tirtamarta dalam Nuansa Kejawen-Kristiani (Serat Suluk Pawestri Samariyah: A quest for living water in Javanese indigenous religion and Christian nuance)', *Diksi* 13(1), 31–42. https://doi.org/10.21831/diksi.v13i1.6434

Purna, I.M., Astuti, R. & Wahyuningsih, 1996, *Macapat dan Gotong Royong (Macapat and Collaboration)*, Direktorat Sejarah dan Nilai Tradisional Direktorat Jenderal Kebudayaan Departemen Pendidikan dan Kebudayaan (Directorate of History and Cultural Values of the Directorate Generale of the Department of Education and Cultural Affairs), Jakarta.

Ricklefs, M., 2006, *Mystic synthesis in Java: A history of Islamization from the fourteenth to the early nineteenth centuries*, Eastbridge Books, Norwalk, CT.

Rukiyah, 2017, 'Ruwatan dalam Masyarakat Jawa (Ruwatan/liberation ritual in Javanese Society)', *Sabda* 3(2), 1–11. https://doi.org/10.14710/sabda.v3i2.13233

Saddhono, K. & Pramestuti, D., 2018, 'Sekar Macapat Pocung: Study of religious values based on the local wisdom of Javanese culture, *El Harakah* 20(1), 15. https://doi. org/10.18860/el.v20i1.4724

Santosa, P., 2016, 'Fungsi Sosial Kemasyarakatan Tembang Macapat (Community Social Functions of Macapat)', *Widyaparwa* 44(2), 97–109. https://doi.org/10. 26499/wdprw.v44i2.138

Sari, M.K., 2021, 'The Reflection of Javanese Cultural Characteristics as Found in English Apology Strategies', *Modality Journal: Journal of International Linguistics and Literature*, 1(1), 36–42.

Sie, S.T., 1923, *Serat Suluk Pawestri Samariyah*, 1st edn., Boekhandel Tan Khoen Swie, Kediri-Solo.

Sie, S.T., 1925, *Serat Suluk Pawestri Samariyah: Anyariyossaken bab toya gesang utawi Tirta marta sarta bab sajatinning pannembah Anggittannipun, Serat Suluk*

Pawestri Samariyah: A story of a quest for living water and true worship to God, AC. Nix & Co, Bandung.

Sie, S.T., 2021, *Serat Suluk Pawestri Samariyah*, transl. J. Sunjoto, Aksara Sinergi Media, Surakarta.

Sukarno, S., 2010, 'The reflection of the Javanese cultural concepts in the politeness of Javanese', K@Ta 12(1), 59–72. https://doi.org/10.9744/kata.12.1.59-71

Suwardi, 2015, 'Wawasan Hidup Jawa dalam Tembang Macapat (Javanese world view in Tembang Macapat)', Diksi 13(5), 1–28. https://doi.org/10.21831/diksi.v13i5.7067

Turnbull, J., 2008, 'Kierkegaard, indirect communication, and ambiguity', The Heythrop Journal 50(1), 13–22. https://doi.org/10.1111/j.1468-2265.2009.00439.x

Van der Merwe, D.G., 2019, 'The divinity of Jesus in the Gospel of John: The "lived experiences" it fostered when the text was read', HTS Teologiese Studies/ Theological Studies 75(1), a5411. https://doi.org/10.4102/hts.v75i1.5411

Zoetmulder, P.J., 1991, *Manunggaling Kawula Gusti, Pantheism and Monisme dalam Sastra Suluk Jawa: suatu studi, filsafat, Mystica Union with the Divine, Pantheism and Monism in Javanese Suluk Literature: A philosphical study*, Gramedia Pustaka Utama, Jakarta.

This work has been published in HTS Teologiese Studies Vol.78, No.4 (2022), with the title:

An Implicit Good News In A Javanese Indigenous Religious Poem.

DOI: https://doi.org/10.4102/hts.v78i4.7403- July 12, 2022.

Homo Viator:
Comparative Study of *Serat Jatimurti* with the Parable of the Prodigal Son

Abstract

Many religions teach various concepts of a spiritual journey. Likewise, the concept of Homo Viator or humans on the person on the journey. This study examines the concept of a spiritual journey in Serat Jatimurti, one of the Javanese Indigenous texts, and compares it with the parable of the Prodigal son in the Bible. This study aims to understand the voice of the local spirituality to facilitate dialogues and an effective effort when someone intends to share the good news with the indigenous spiritual communities. By using cognitive linguistic analysis, the results show some similarities and differences in those texts. The similarities in those texts might increase appreciation of each spirituality as they might become a common ground for in-depth communication. Then, the differences can help various religious adherents to reflect on the uniqueness of their belief. Meanwhile, for the Christians, the differences can help to define the core of the good news for the process of sharing it with the followers of the Javanese indigenous spirituality while also listening to their voices.

Keywords: Homo Viator, Indigenous spirituality, Spiritual Journey Metaphors, and Cognitive Linguistics

Introduction

The spiritual journey concept exists in many religions. The spiritual masters of the indigenous spiritual communities in Indonesia also teach the concept. Although the formal name of those communities is Penghayat, many people might name them Kebatinan, or Kejawen. In their concept, first, humans are travellers or pilgrims in their spiritual life. He emphasizes "After completing the errands there, we quickly return home."(Endraswara 2006:45) They use the phrase *wong urip iku mung mampir ngombe* which means that life is like a time to stop by only to drink. (Kasnadi & Sutejo 2018:41) Similarly, Sunan Kalijaga, one of the Wali Songo who popularly is considered the most prominent Javenses-Islamic mystic creates a poem that teaches about life in this world as a trip to a market. The market is not a final destination. Second, it is popular that many indigenous spiritual leaders view life as a long path to be walked through with many phases. In Central and East Java, such a view is well known. Analysing the phrase signifies that for the Javanese indigenous spiritual adherents, the spiritual journey is the process to move to leaving the temporal reality and progressing to a destination where eternity or true reality exists.

At the beginning of the 20th century, a Javanese literary text was published. The title is *Serat Jatimurti* which means the letter of Truth. It was written by R. Soedjonoredjo. Theodor Pigeaud, a well-known Javanese culture and literature scholar writes a book to describe that such a text and other Javanese literature of the early 20th century are classified as the new revival of classical Javanese literature. (Pigeaud 1967) Many researchers such as Asmara, have analysed those texts either from metaphysical, spirituality, or literature and comparative religion framework. (Asmara 2013)

In this study, the spiritual journey concept of *Serat Jatimurti* is compared with the parable of the prodigal son of Luke 15:11-32. The prodigal son as a narrative has been inspiring many Christian circles and caused many scholars to study it as a metaphor for a spiritual journey. Timothy Keller even concludes that the parable point to the core of the Christian faith. (Keller 2008) Another expert, Burke, in his study of the metaphors in the parable states that the metaphor teaches that God is like a father who waits for human beings in love, forgiveness and grace of new life. (Burke 2013)

The study chooses S*erat Jatimurti* among similar Javanese texts as Serat Centini, Gatolotjo, and others based on its uniqueness. First, the language that the writer of *Serat Jatimurti* uses is Javanese which ordinary people use daily. It is called *ngoko* language. This fact is unusual as most Javanese literature uses a high and sophisticated language called *kromo inggil*. This uniqueness of Serat Jatimurti might indicate the writer's intention that his work can be accessed and understood by ordinary people. This phenomenon is unusual as at the beginning of the 20th century the Javanese society was rather feudalistic and hierarchical. Not many spiritual leaders wished to share their exoteric indigenous spiritual teachings with society except for the chosen one. The choice of Soedjonoredjo as such might have caused the fact that a spiritual community, *Hardo Pusara* where he originated still exist in various places today. Second. *Serat Jatimurti* combines direct expressions or sentences with many figurative languages mainly metaphors. Many times, the direct sentences are dialectical, something that indicates the view of the writer concerning the complexity and multidimensionality of reality. Such a view is more stands out when he describes the process that human beings undergo toward the union with the Divine. Third, there has not been any study done to compare the concept of the spiritual journey in *Serat Jatimurti* with the metaphorical interpretation of the parable of the prodigal son, an approach that treats it as a set of metaphors and embedded teaching about the roles of the *Homo Viator,* or humans on a journey.

Furthermore, the basis for choosing the parable of the prodigal son lies in the fact that the narrative has been widely treated or interpreted as a metaphor for a spiritual journey. For example, Aurel Lehaci Onicim from University Bucharest states that the parable points to the prodigal son's spiritual journey from being a sinner to becoming a Viator and returning to union with God, the Father. (Onisim 2017) The rich dimension of this parable has become the primary material of various novels, dramas, poems, paintings, or statues that convey its richness until today as described by Alison Jack (Jack 2019) and Pietro Delcorno. (Delcorno 2017)

The parable has also been studied by scholars to analyse its voice concerning the Father who has been losing two sons. (Young 2008:138) It is a fact that the father also lost his oldest son as he does not support the unconditional grace, forgiveness, reconciliation, and total recovery that the old man gives. (Onisim 2017:140) Clark-King concludes that the parable of the prodigal son teaches the core of

Christian values which is forgiveness of God which is given unconditionally that each human in their inner life needs and longs for. (Clark-King 2007:238)

The contribution intended by this work on *Serat Jatimurti* and the parable of the prodigal son is based that the comparative study on them might equip adherents of different spiritual communities to learn about each other and appreciate them, while simultaneously delving deeper into the core of the beliefs that become their spiritual foundation. If they learn and discover some similarities in the process of dialogue, such findings might serve as a *common ground* or bridge that effectively opens a healthy relationship. For Christians, learning about the differences in the concept of the spiritual journey might become a door for them to share their spiritual insight. They might be able to share the good news by using others' patterns of thought and communication styles. Thus, others can learn about the attractiveness of the grace of God.

Methodology

The qualitative method is used in this study. For the data analysis, the study uses Cognitive linguistics theory as the basis to explore the metaphors in *Serat Jatimurt*i and the parable of the prodigal son which is treated as a set of metaphors. Metaphors belong to figurative language as described by Evans and Green. (Evans & Green 2006) In this approach, the concrete aspects of each metaphor which communicate things that the readers are familiar with will be interpreted to understand the teachings that each metaphor points out and is contained in the abstract domain or the hidden aspects of the metaphor.

Thus, what the Cognitive linguistic theory names the concrete domain of the journey metaphor that *Serat Jatimurti* contains will be analysed to discover the things that people are familiar with and each metaphor emphasizes. From the result of the analysis, its spiritual teaching will be concluded. With a similar approach, there will be an analysis done on the journey of the prodigal son as *Homo Viator*. Analysis of Luke 15:11–32 will focus to uncover the concrete and abstract domains of the journey stages of the prodigal son. Then lastly, based on those results, the writer will compare *Serat Jatimurti* with the parable of the prodigal son mainly the focus is on the stages of the spiritual journey, the roles of human beings as *Homo Viator*, and each concept of God.

The Result and Discussion

Spiritual Journey Metaphor of *Homo Viator*

In the West, one of the popular terms is *Homo Viator*. It means that humans are viewed as *Homo Viator* which means the travellers on one who is on a journey. Nauta ties the life of Agustinus, theologian and Church Father of the fourth century with the term to describe his turning point and spiritual progression. (Nauta 2008) One of the philosophers, Gabriel Marcel, also writes a book entitled *Homo Viator*. In the book, he writes that stability will exist in the world if human beings always remember their existence as pilgrims. (Sweetman 2012) Books and articles that describe human beings as pilgrims or travellers keep on adding, a fact that signifies that the journey metaphor is universally accepted and used due to its rich dimensions, for example, the articles written by Vos (Vos 2014) or Barbato. (Barbato 2016)

To analyse the text of *Serat Jatimurti*, first, this study poses questions such as "who is the Homo Viator in that text?" Secondly, How could humans start the spiritual journey? Third, what is the destination of the journey that humans try to achieve? What are the stages of the journey that he or she has to pass through?

By uncovering the hidden aspects or embedded concepts in each metaphor, the total spiritual concept or the teachings of *Serat Jatimurti* could be identified. With the results, mainly about the identity and essence of *Homo Viator* according to the concept of Soedjonoredjo, the journey stages, and the destination, the whole teaching of this indigenous Javanese text will be compared with the teaching of the parable of the Prodigal son that the metaphors convey.

The Background of *Serat Jatimurti*

Serat means a written paper or a paper that contains a certain thing. *Jati* means something genuine, true, or the essence of everything, while *Murti* means appearance or forms. (Prawiroadmojo 1989) In short, *Serat Jatimurti* means a text about Genuine Reality or Truth. The writer of this text, Raden Soedjonoredjo is a schoolmaster. In his era, with such a profession, he should have mastered the Dutch language, Javanese language, and Malay. It means that he is an educated person who is well-respected by most Javanese. However, the Dutch Colonial officers might underestimate him as a member of indigenous society, especially, since his spirituality does not receive recognition by most educated Europeans. Until today, even many Indonesians view their indigenous spirituality and community as illogical and superstitious,

He creates *Serat Jatimurti* to communicate his spiritual insights concerning *kasunyatan* (the true Reality). Beforehand, he learns from Ki Soemotjitro, a master of mystics who develops *Hardo Pusara* mystical community. *Hardo Pusara* teaches methods on how to control human sensory perception and thus enable them to journey toward a state of perfection. This community and its spirituality becomes a formal organization in 1910 and even today has many branches and followers in central Java. (Soemotjitro & Direktorat Jendral Kebudayaan 1980)

During the colonial era, Java communities were coloured heavily by hierarchical feudalistic, and paternalistic culture. Masters or gurus share their spiritual teaching which they consider secret knowledge to be communicated only to the chosen people. Therefore, they used high-level language and took the form of sophisticated poems or songs. Soedjonoredjo's decision to write his spiritual teaching in a common language is unusual in his era. Siswanto states that his choice is based on his wish to share his wisdom or spiritual insights with as many people as he could instead of with a limited number of Javanese society members. (Siswanto 2016) In his study, he points to the main feature of the text which is metaphysical philosophy. Concerning the content, Nicolas Girardet writes that essentially *Serat Jatimurti* is a mystical text about creation, existence, God, spirit, and soul. (Kratz 1985) *Serat Jatimurti* begins its teaching with an emphasis on reality and the human journey through many domains in it to progress toward the True Reality or God.

The Background of the Parable of Prodigal son
In the Bible, there are many parables and metaphors. They are used to convey teachings about moral standards or principles of faith life. The parable of the Prodigal son in Luke 15 can also be considered as an expanded metaphor in a form of narrative. (Naseri 2017) That parable is a part of a set of parables consisting of the parable of the Lost Lamb and the parable of the Lost coin. In the gospel of Luke, Jesus teaches such parables to reply to the criticisms of the Pharisees and the Scribes concerning His action and ministry. At a glance, the

parables are to convey the Lord's teaching about the presence of happiness when something missing has returned. The lamb is cattle, the coin signified treasure, and the son relates to reputation, descendant, and close relationship. All of them are very valuable in such a way that when they are lost the impact is significant and when they come back, real happiness appears.

According to Alles, this parable is a description based on a real event in life. By using the Cognitive linguistics theory, the starting point exists in the concrete domain of life or aspects that people are familiar with. (Alles, Tyrell 2008:14) In this domain, there are many aspects such as family, ethics, and journey. Christopher Naseri states that Biblical scholars have studied and looked for a more accurate title for the parable as it has two characters like contrasting elements: the prodigal and the oldest son. (Naseri 2017) Therefore, although the original title is "the Lost Son" many scholars propose different titles. For example, Allan Culpepper suggests *"The Prodigal son, the Compassionate Father and, the Angry Brother"* for the parable because there are emphases on the characters of the father and the oldest son beside the youngest one. (Culpepper 1995:3) Through the response of each of them especially to the return of the prodigal son, the parable conveys an embedded teaching or an abstract concept. Thus, the title "the Lost Son" is not sufficient to signify the message or structure of the narrative behind the two characters that are compared as such. (Naseri 2017:149)

In general, scholars agree that at least this parable has three meanings. First, this parable teaches the character of God as the Father who has unlimited love that no other father in the world loves and acts. (Fitzmyer 1981) Second, through the parable, Jesus wishes to show the importance of His ministry to the marginalized people as a reply to the criticism of the Pharisees and the Scribes. (Hultgren & J. 2000:85–86) Third, through the parable, Jesus also intends to teach them that the Kingdom of God has arrived through His ministry and acts—something to be welcomed with joy and celebration when the lost ones respond positively to the Gospel. repent, and return to God. (Alles, Tyrell 2008:21–22) Furthermore, according to the ethnic-based interpretations of Tertullian and Augustine, the oldest son in the parable depicts the Jews who hear about Christ but reject Him while the youngest is the gentiles who receive grace in Christ. (Baltes 2018:278–282)

For those who study the interpretation of the parable, there are wide varieties of them to be used due to the richness and multi-dimension of the narrative. Yet there is something that seldom becomes the focal point of the interpretations. It is the journey process of the Prodigal son away from the home and later decides to return as a metaphor for the human spiritual journey.

The study of Lehaci Onisim, *The Parable of the Prodigal son: A Cognitive Linguistic Analysis* proposes such a focus. In his article, the journey is treated as the concrete domain that signifies the turning point, hindrance, progress, or regress, and the final destination. (Onisim 2017:146) A similar view is also conveyed by other scholars such as Linnemann, who views the journey of the Prodigal son as a journey into sin, death, and then returning process to a new life based on the sentence in Luke: "My son has died and lived again, lost and found again. (Linnemann 1986)

With such an approach, the interpretation of the Prodigal son parable can explain more the abstract or embedded teaching: there are some difficult steps in the journey home. First, the Prodigal son has to enter a process of self-transformation when he decides to return to his father rather than stay in the location that originally serves as his destination. In the concrete domain, it is described that when he left home, he carries a large amount of money. Oppositely, when he decides to return home, he has to endure hunger, poverty, and physical discomfort as he does not even has footwear, something that his profession demands in that era. From the words that he says to himself, the Prodigal son arrives at an awareness that his decision and action to leave home has neglected the expectation of his father. The returning process demands a strong motivation and willingness to pay the price.

Second, from the point of his decision to return home and during the difficult journey home, he has to struggle continuously with the possibility that his father or his family might reject him as he has caused embarrassment. Exploring the parable with this approach will yield insights concerning the stages and hindrances that someone who decides to undergo a spiritual journey or become *Homo Viator* has to experience before he experiences a union with God.

Textual Analysis of the Journey Metaphor in *Serat Jatimurti*

Metaphors of the Journey and the Locations
The opening sentence of *Serat Jatimurti* states that, "*Rehning ana Kahanan Jati, iya ana kahanan kang ora jati. Barang kang ana iku temene maune mula ana. Sing ora ana, maune ya ora ana.*" (Soedjonoredjo 1980) The translation of the sentence is: "Truly, there is a true reality and there is a false one. What truly exists has been there since the beginning. What does not exist is non-exist from the beginning." This first sentence of the text is multi-interpretable and very abstract. The word "exist" or " "ana" in the Javanese language can be understood in many different ways. The sentence might mean that there is a genuine reality but also there is a false or illusive reality. The true reality exists from the beginning while the false one only later emerges.

In short, embedded in this sentence *Serat Jatimurti* posits that there is a primary reality and the true one. As a comparison, the text also teaches that there is a false or fabricated reality. In the following sentences, *Serat Jatimurti* indicates that only God is the true reality. The term "God" in *Serat Jatimurti* is Allah instead of *Gusti, or Hyang Manon* the terms that the Javanese ordinarily use to address God. The term indicates that socially Soedjonoredjo has adopted Islam as his religion even though he never abandons his original indigenous spirituality. (Soedjonoredjo 1980:11)

Continuing his description of reality, Soedjonoredjo uses three metaphors to explain what humans have to do in a reality that keeps on fluctuating, changing, and untrue. He states that

Donya iku dalan, iya kudu diambah apa mesthine. Nangun dudu benere yen dirungkebana. Sing sapa ngambah dalan, kudu sumurup, yen kang ana ing sangarepe, sanajan diparanana, mung bakal dilewati bae.(Soedjonoredjo 1980:11)

The sentence means "the World is a path, has to be walked through properly. What we pass through is not the destination. Whoever walkthrough has to realize that whatever is in his or her front is not the destination but to be left behind."

Then, the writer describes three spheres that humans have to approach, enter, and pass through. They are called the line sphere, surface sphere, and then the form sphere. Soedjonoredjo describes those three spheres by connecting them with a human hand. They are then, the line, the palm, and the whole. He describes humans as tiny creatures as big as a dot who crawls on the large hand palm. Thus far, the depiction of reality as a hand palm is not widely used in Indonesia or the West. Only Hui Fan has done a study on the metaphors and allegories of hand in Chinese culture. (Fan 2017)

The Journey in the Line Sphere
For Soedjonoredjo, each journey has to have a starting point. In *Serat Jatimurti*, the journey begins with someone who exists in the line sphere. The term line sphere means a reality where humans work and live. Its feature is as Soedjonoredjo describes:

Alam Garis iku banget enggone rupek. Kang lungguh ing Alam Garis yaiku cecek, si cecek kang ana ing alame mau mung nurut enggon sauruting garis. Lire mung maju karo mundur, ora ana keblat kiwa lan tengen, mung ngarep lan mburi. Dadi cecek mau ora duwe cara nyimpang. Mulane upama si cecek dicegat ngarep lan mburi, ora oleh panggonan maneh, kejaba yen banjur manjing ing alam lumah. Dene bisane manjing ing alam lumah menawa salin wujud kang manut caraning lumah, tegese arupa lumah ciyut utawa bunderan lembut, dadi wis ora wujud ceceking garis, nanging manggon ing lumah.(Soedjonoredjo 1980:16)

The translation of the sentence is: "The line sphere is very narrow. Whoever stays there only dots. Dots stay along the line. Either go forward or backwards, cannot go sideway to the left or right. Therefore, when the dot faces an obstacle in the front or back, it can only move to the left or right and it enters the surface sphere. It should walk on the forms of the surface, it does not form a line together with other dots. It will become a small circle while the form of line disappears."

Interpreting the meaning of the sentences related to the metaphor of the line sphere is not difficult. In the line sphere, humans are described as playing roles as dots in their lives. They could not do much except for following other dots to form a line and move along the line of a hand palm.

After explaining the tiny humans as dots or bacteria, Soedjonoredjo asks a strange question, "Does a line consist of dots?" The question brings people to the realization that according to *Serat Jatimurti*, the line that the dots follow does not exist. The line is the reality that dots' perception creates which also causes them to walk on. Furthermore, the dots are not related to becoming a solid line as each of them is separated from the others. This metaphor indicates that the reality of life only exists the in the perception of human beings. It also means that in the line sphere, each person as dot centres on him or herself while following the crowds. They also push each other but only along a line that the human mind creates.

By using the Cognitive Linguistic Analysis of the concrete domain of this metaphor, this study identifies its stand-out aspects. The metaphor emphasizes the following. First, as travellers, humans are *Homo Viator* who are driven to follow only a path based on what their mind perceives as reality. With or without realizing it, they are driven also by other people who walk behind them. Thus, being *Homo Viator* humans play the role of the ones who adjust themselves to others or follow the crowd. The hidden teaching of the metaphor is as follows. First, humans can realize that they are on a journey. Second, they have also the capacity to choose their responses to the reality that they perceive. Then, lastly, in this sphere, as *Homo Viator* humans follow their self-will.

The Journey in the Surface Sphere
After the line sphere, humans can enter, walk, and progress in the second sphere which is the surface sphere. The surface sphere metaphor points out that this sphere is wider, has more space, and offers more freedom for those who walk in it. The metaphor that *Serat Jatimurti* uses is a hand palm which is a surface that has many lines. The feature of this surface sphere is written in *Serat Jatimurti* as follows: "*Alam lumah luwih jembar tinimbang Alam Garis, sebab ing alam lumah ora, mung ana ngarep karo buri bae, uga ana keblat kiwa sarta tengen.*"(Soedjonoredjo 1980:17) The surface sphere allows the traveller to walk to the left or right side.

Serat Jatimurti also describes that this second sphere consists of many lines and thus relates to the first sphere which is the line sphere. In the surface sphere, humans' sensory perception plays the role to define something as valuable or not. Then, they pursue them, but once they cannot move again, they stop. For example, they walk until arriving at the edge of the hand palm. Soedjonoredjo emphasizes that in the second sphere humans have freedom but cannot walk upward or downward. He also states, *"marga ing alam lumah ora ana keblat ngisor lan dhuwur"*(Soedjonoredjo 1980:17) which means "because, in the surface sphere, there is no path upward or downward."

Cognitive Linguistic Analysis of the metaphor identifies the hidden and highlighted aspects of the metaphor. The highlighted ones are as follows. First, humans as *Homo Viator* are driven to step out from the path or line that they perceive as the true reality. Thus, in this stage of the journey, *Homo Viator* plays the role of a person who dares to find his or her path instead of following the crowd. Second, at this stage of the journey, humans focus on the surface but they do not dare to go further especially to explore the surface under the hand palm. Third, the direction that they pursue in the journey is something they like.

In this stage of the journey, the hidden aspects of the metaphor are (1) the capacity of human beings to realize their journey; (2) the ability of human beings to go through the limit.; and (3) the hindrance or obstacle to moving forward lies in the humans' inner motivation to centre on their self-needs as *Homo Viator*.

Journey in the Form Sphere (*Jirim*)
When journeying in the third sphere, the *Jirim* sphere, humans realize that this sphere is extremely wider and larger than the first two spheres that they have walked through. *Jirim* means matter or form. This sphere contains both lines and surfaces as it is three-dimensional. Therefore, humans who journey here can move backwards, frontward, sideways, or upward and downward. They could even move diagonally. In *Serat Jatimurti*, a human hand or fist becomes the symbol or metaphor of this sphere.

In this wide sphere, humans can even develop themselves. If in the first two spheres they were controlled by their limited intuition or perception, at this new stage of the journey they learn to realize that they have more possibilities or choices that they can have. They can even change many of their habits as written in the text.

> *Alam Jirim luwih jembar tebane katimbang alam lumah, awit ora mung duwe keblat ngarep mburi lan kiwa tengen bae, uga duwe keblat ngisor*

lan dhuwur. Mulane yen jisim kinubengan ing garis temu gelang, isih oleh panggonan yang jembar. Awit bisa munggah mudhun, mangiwa manengen, maju mundur, ngewas mangiwa lan manengen, ngewas mandhuwur lan mangisor. Sakarepkarep kaya dene aburing laler utawa nglangining iwak.(Soedjonoredjo 1980:17–18)

The translation of the text is: "The Form Sphere is much wider than the surface sphere as there are paths to go not only backwards or frontwards, left or right, but also upwards and downwards. The sphere is like a big circle, the dot can move freely like a fly or swimming fish."

Thus in this stage of the journey, they learn to abandon whatever they used to perceive as absolute or something valuable to be pursued during the journey in the line or surface spheres. However, humans in the Form Sphere are still attached or bound in time and space. Only in the fourth sphere which is the destination of the journey, does time or space become non-exist.

Analysis of the metaphor in this third stage of the journey shows that there are highlighted and hidden aspects. The hidden aspect indicates the teaching of Soedjonoredjo. In the highlighted aspects the teachings can be described: First, as *Homo Viator* at this stage humans are driven to journey simply to fulfil their own needs, wishes, and perception, but they learn to choose a new way as a step to be liberated from the previous self-bondage. Thus, at this stage, humans learn to play their roles as humans who dare to uncover something meaningful. Second, the path of the journey that they choose brings them to the realization of the three-dimensional sphere. Third, the goal to be pursued in this journey is to gain perfection and live with virtues. Thus, the message of the text is (1) that even in this sphere humans are still attached to space; (2) humans are still bound by time; (3) and humans could be trapped to enjoy the unlimited space in this sphere.

Arriving at the True Reality as The Destination of the Journey
In *Serat Jatimurti*, Soedjonoredjo names the fourth sphere as *Kahanan Jati* or the True Reality. As has been described above, there is no time or space in this *Kahanan Jati*. Nothing is comparable to its width and volume. There is no metaphor to be used to describe it. It is then, beyond human language to fathom and express its feature. Therefore, *Serat Jatimurti* combines linear expressions that can be multi-interpretable, abstract, and even dialectical as an effort to give

hints about its features. For example, first, in describing the fourth sphere, *Serat Jatimurti* states that this sphere is "unlimited." No human word suffices to describe it. Thus, Soedjonoredjo means to convey that no human can explain the fourth sphere adequately.

Yet, after giving such a statement he adds the second statement. *Kahanan Jati* does not need space and time, even all space and time in the universe are controlled by *Kahanan Jati*. In *Serat Jatimurti*, it is stated that *Kahanan Jati* or True Reality is God as God created time and space to manifest God-self in the sphere of line, surface, and form. Whether is manifestation concept of Soedjonoredjo similar to the concept of Divine emanation in the West might need more theological exploration or analysis. It is then interesting that Soedjonoredjo gives two different or might be opposite statements. On the one hand, humans could not explain and describe this final destination of the spiritual journey. It means that on the one hand, most people could not understand and speak about it. On the other hand, as a human being, Soedjonoredjo could describe and write about it. It might mean that for him, most people are incapable to explain the *Kahanan Jati*, but only limited persons can describe it after they have experienced a mystical union with the Divine who will then endow them with such capability.

From the analyses of the metaphors of *Serat Jatimurti*, it can be concluded that in them there is an embedded concept of humans as *Homo Viator* who in the first stage of their spiritual journey only have limited capability, but along the way, there is progress as they learn to recognize many choices in the wider sphere. A question remains. How could humans arrive at the realization of the existence of *Kahanan Jati*? The analysis shows that no human could recognize the existence of *Kahanan Jati* based on their sensory perception only. They need another starting point.

In *Serat Jatimurti*, the journey as *Homo Viator* can take place as essentially, the human soul is the spark of the Divine. This essence enables humans to choose between taking sides with their lust, wishes, needs, and self-centredness or abandoning them and stepping into a process toward union with God. The divine spark enables them to control or dampen the drive that roots in emotion and sensory perception that might trap them either only in the Line Sphere, the Surface Sphere, or the Form Space. Thus, the starting point for the whole journey is to allow quietness, peace, and serenity to enter the human soul, master it, and train to have sensitivity.

Analysing the Parable of The Prodigal son as a Journey Metaphor

The prodigal son parable begins with a narrative of a family that consists of a father and two sons as the main characters. The youngest son demands the father give him his inheritance. After it is given, he goes to a faraway place. There he lives according to his wishes. After he spends all his inheritance, a famine takes place. In such a condition, he does not return home but stays and struggles to survive. He hires himself out as a pig feeder. In that era, that job is a low-status one, only a slave is lower. Yet, even though he works hard and struggles, the income from his job does not provide enough for him. He suffers continuous hunger and no one helps him. At that point, he reflects on his life journey and then, speaks inwardly to himself. He decides to return to his father. The intention is to confess his mistakes and asks for forgiveness then, applies for a job on his father's estate. After he walks through a difficult journey, not only the father accepts and forgives him, but also provides a new robe, sandals, and rings. He even instructs the young son to party because the father wants people to know his happiness as his son has returned home. Afterwards, the narrative shifts to highlight the responses of the oldest son who could not accept his returning sibling.

In the parable, it is evident that the concrete domain of the journey metaphor points out that, it all begins with the young son's initiative. It also highlights the fact that the whole journey, including the beginning and turning point, consists of three stages as follows.

The first stage of the journey takes place when the prodigal son lives in the house of his father. Several highlighted aspects appear in this journey metaphor as uncovered by a few studies such as done by Snodgrass or Hultgren. First, the youngest son dares to take a choice and bold initiative. Snodgrass mentions that in their culture at that time, it is a deviation from normalcy that a child asks to leave his home as most fathers wish to raise their children until they reach adulthood and live or work around then, continue their work. In the farming community, the status of a farmer is well respected. Leaving the honoured status and job means erasing the community's respect and bringing shame to the family.

(Klyne Snodgrass 2018:109) Second, the youngest son has a dream or destination that he pursues in his journey. Third, he is capable to obtain what he wants and executing his plan.

The hidden aspects of this first stage of the journey are evident. First, in the Jewish culture, the youngest son's action to claim or demand his inheritance is extraordinarily improper. Asking for his inheritance and leaving his family means that he takes the treasure that is supposed to be used to care for the life of his father later. By doing so he ignores his responsibility to take care of his father when the old man gets older. (Klyne Snodgrass 2018:109)It also means that by leaving his family, he has disregarded the opinion of his father who might have advised him concerning his decision. Even more, according to Hultgren, the youngest son's action shows that he has chosen not only physically distances himself from his family but psychologically he cut his ties with the community where he originates. In short, according to Snodgrass, the youngest son has prepared himself to be no longer recognized as a member of the family by his father. (Klyne Snodgrass 2018:109)

The second stage of the journey consists of many events that take place after he arrives at the country that becomes his destination. In this second stage of the journey, the metaphor emphasizes several aspects that stand out as follows. In the beginning, the youngest son lives with his friends and enjoys life. Later, there is a disruption with the arrival of famine. In that situation, he has squandered his money. He struggles and tries to find a solution. However, the solution does not yield results according to his plan. He suffers from poverty, low social status, and even continuous hunger.

There are some hidden aspects in the concrete domain of the second stage of the journey metaphor. The prodigal son lives as a pig feeder, a low status. In the Jewish community, a pig feeder is almost the same status as a slave. A scholar, Nasen mentions that it is common that pig feeders not allowed to wear shoes or sandals. (Naseri 2017:152) However, despite the hardship, the prodigal son proves that he is a tough person in dealing with the consequences of his wrong choice by surviving extreme poverty and physical suffering.

In the third stage of the journey, there is a turning point experience. It takes place when he works as the pig feeder. He evaluates himself and makes a deep reflection. At that point, he remembers his father's home. In his mind, he realizes his wrongdoing. He calculates that working as an employee at his father's house is better than becoming a pig feeder in a faraway country. Then, he decides to start his journey home to admit his mistakes. He must have realized that the long journey might entail risk and consequences. His father might refuse or reject him completely due to the embarrassment that he causes. Despite such a possibility, he wants to fix his relationship with his father and admit his self-centeredness.

The hidden aspects of the third stage of the journey are hard to recognize if one does not know the context. The journey home will become an arduous and painful journey as he has to walk barefoot while enduring hunger and poverty. He might also face his neighbours' insults when he passes down the road in front of their houses.

The fourth stage of the journey is the encounter between the father and the son. A union takes place. The highlighted aspects of the parable show that the father has seen the son from a distance and then he runs to welcome him. He embraces and kisses the prodigal son who must smell bad like pigs, hungry, and dishevelled. Despite the embarrassment and the loss of treasure the son has caused, the father shows his unconditional welcome. He even gives the son a ring which is a symbol of power, a new robe which might be understood or indicates a new status, and footwear which means protection. The conclusion to be drawn from the highlighted points, the father gives reconciliation, forgiveness, and unconditional grace to the lost son who has returned home and causes happiness or joy for the father.

The hidden aspects in the fourth stage of the journey are clear. The father emphasizes reconciliation in the relationship with his sons rather than keeping a tab on his wrong choices and the cost. The father gives the returning son not only food and work, but also unconditional acceptance, renewed status, new opportunity, protection, and even assignment.

Similarities and Differences in the Journey Metaphors of *Serat Jatimurti* and The Parable of the Prodigal son

By comparing the metaphor of *Serat Jatimurti* and the parable of the Prodigal son, besides the similarities, there are many contrasting concepts. All of them signify some universal views on reality, or spiritual journey, and some differences.

First, Serat Jatimurti and the parable of the Prodigal son similarly describe the spiritual journey of humans as *Homo Viator*. Second, both describe the spiritual journey consists of four stages that the dot and the prodigal son have to undergo. Third, the returning journey to God begins to take place when the human makes reflection and evaluates his or her reality including the experiences of passing through the previous journeys. According to *Serat Jatimurti*, the starting point of the returning journey to God takes place when humans choose to enter quietness and enjoy the serenity. In such a condition, they become aware of the existence of the True Reality and the perceived one which their mind creates. From then on, they learn to control their self-centredness or wishes. The same teaching is also embedded in the parable of the prodigal son when the main character evaluates his misery. Both teachings are even similar to the teaching of the Sufi, some Hindu views or, Buddhist teaching. Thus, it can be concluded that all religions remind human beings to realize the needs and importance of having a stop, reflecting, and entering quietness to start the journey toward the Divine.

Besides the results of those analyses that point to three similarities, there are also some differences. First, in teaching about the starting point of the journey to the Divine union, there are contrasting views. As *Serat Jatimurti* does not propose any concept of sin and grace, therefore, it teaches that humans can make a choice either entering a spiritual journey and arriving at the destination which is experiencing the True Reality or deciding to continue living in the illusive reality. Humans have such a capability as *Serat Jatimurti* views that essentially they have the Divine spark in their soul. Such a view is common in the Javanese indigenous mystic spirituality. (Endraswara 2006:65)

Different from *Serat Jatimurti,* the parable of the prodigal son highlights the turning point of the main character when he decides to start his returning journey to his father. The turning point is related to his evaluation and reflection of his miseries and inability to solve his problems. The decision of the prodigal son begins with his evaluation and honest admittance of his inability to save or liberate himself from poverty and hunger. He also realizes his sin to his God and father. In his desperation, he experiences transformation in his perception and perspective of life. Before that moment, he lives with limited knowledge of his father, self-centeredness and materialism, then the reflection brings him to perceive his father deeper as a generous master to his employees. He gives them enough food or even abundantly. Daily workers at that time are the poorest citizen. In comparison, slaves who live and work in the house of their masters have regular food and a place to stay. The daily workers do not have a regular income but depend on the work that gets each day (comp. Mat. 20:1–16). Therefore, according to the Torah, God instructs the Israelites not to withhold the salary of their daily workers (Leviticus. 19:13). Now, the prodigal son has a real personal experience of the daily workers' suffering.

Therefore, based on such realization and new perspective he chooses to start his journey home. Somehow, in the parable, the suffering and failure of the prodigal son trigger him to have a turning point and to a new choice. The parable indicates that making choices is important in a spiritual journey while *Serat Jatimurti* does not emphasize pain, suffering, poverty, failure, or hunger as the trigger for the emerging awareness. The text simply shows that humans are trapped in the journey in the illusive reality without describing the root of being in such a condition. A human simply has a journey in the wrong place or illusion, a journey that relies on their perception.

Second, although *Serat Jatimurti* and the parable of the Prodigal son similarly point to the journey stages and the destination, there is a difference in the union with the Divine concept. In *Serat Jatimurti*, at that union or *Unio Mystica,* the human identity disappears as it merges completely with God. Such a view is widely spread in the Javanese indigenous beliefs. (Endraswara 2006:46–50) In comparison, in the parable of Prodigal son, the *Unio Mystica* is more like *communion* or a condition where the father and the son embrace each other, but each of their identity is intact and does not disappear.

Third, according to *Serat Jatimurti*, the obstacles that exist in the journey process are caused by human's tendency to continuously rely on or trust their perception and self-centeredness. Meanwhile, in the parable of the prodigal son, the potential obstacle in the returning journey is the suffering and pains in the journey that he has to endure. He has to be well-prepared to endure insults as people in the society where his home exists might look down and scold him. He might have to be ready to receive stones that people cast on him (compared with Deuteronomy 21:18–21). He might also face his father's rejection. However, his commitment is strong: "I will raise and go back to my father... there he wakes up and goes the father." Embarrassment, pain, and punishment do not become a hindrance for him to beg for his father's forgiveness.

Fourth, in *Serat Jatimurti*, the Divine is an abstract Creator. In the parable of the prodigal son, God is depicted as more concrete or a person who is active and takes initiative. God also gives conditional grace. God is like a father who gives inheritance, allows his son to make a choice, offers forgiveness, and shows compassion. God is also a person who gives humans a certain role by having a robe, ring, footwear, and instruction to party after being accepted. Thus, through the parable of the prodigal son, Jesus shows the figure of God who is generous, and who waits patiently for sinful humans to repent or receive the Divine Grace. As communion takes place, God has great joy as the lost one has been found (Luke 15:7, 10, 32). A researcher, Susanto, the Divine Figure in Jesus who seeks and saves the lost one relates to the social dimension of the gospel of Luke that gives special attention to the marginals. (Susanto 2020) Thus, an abstract concept of God in *Serat Jatimurti* is apparent as the anthropomorphic concept of God in the parable of the prodigal son.

The Implication for Dialogues and Sharing the Good News

From the exploration and textual interpretation or analysis, metaphors and parables can be used as effective means to bridge the relationship between different spiritualities. Christians could use the finding to share the good news with the adherents of the indigenous spiritualities. As the Javanese indigenous spirituality adherents believe that the Divine is beyond human languages to describe, those who want to share the good news should depend much on the use of direct language, declaration, or logical explanation in the communication process and relationship building. The indigenous spirituality adherents might consider that an anthropomorphic God does not limit their understanding of God that is beyond human words but completes it.

Practically, the sharing process between various spiritualities should undergo several stages. Those who want to share the good news should come closer and live with them. They have to make the recipient of the good news feel comfortable with them. What Philips does in the process of communicating the Gospel to the Ethiopian eunuch can serve as a model (the Book of Acts. 8:31).

Second, after they get familiar with each other, verbal communication can be started. At this stage, acknowledging the similar view that the spiritual journey is important in human life can become the starting point of discussion. The use of simple or common folk language can be added with figurative language such as metaphors that both parties are familiar with. Also at this point, both of them can share their beliefs and spiritual insights especially, accepting the fact that human language and words are limited to be used to describe God and the human spiritual journey in detail.

Third, as each side perceives their beliefs are respected and honours, with the similarities that each recognizes, several questions concerning the Divine can be asked especially, for the indigenous spirituality adherents. Afterwards, some possibilities of the answers to the questions can be offered to be explored together. Then, the indigenous spirituality adherents can be offered to hear the good news about God's grace and sin.

It must be difficult, but they might be offered to hear about the concept of sin and redemption. Christians who choose this approach for sharing the good news should at this stage share their spiritual journey primarily about the experience of the grace of God. In the fourth stage as a climax, when God gives the moment, the Christians might introduce Jesus Christ gradually to them. The cross might touch their heart as it manifests the deed of emptying oneself for God.

The comparative analysis of *Serat Jatimurti* and the parable of the Prodigal son by using the Cognitive Linguistic Analysis shows many explicit aspects as well as abstract ones. In the concrete and abstract domains of each text, it is evident that there are similarities in the journey metaphors which consist of starting point or turning point, stages, and destination. The significant differences are also recognizable as *Serat Jatimurti* describes the Divine as mysterious and abstract while the parable of the Prodigal son points to the figure of God who has a personality that is full of love and compassion even, cares to incarnate to the world to redeem the humans from their sin. *Serat Jatimurti* does not speak about sin and grace, but the parable of the Prodigal son emphasizes the presence of sin and the need for God's unconditional grace. The similarities in those texts can become the *common ground* for positive communication while the differences can be used to introduce the indigenous spirituality adherents to the good news in Christ.

References

Alles, Tyrell, J., 2008, *The narrative meaning and function of the Parable of the Prodigal Son (Luke 15:11–32)* – PhD thesis, The Catholic University of America.

Asmara, A., 2013, 'Dimensi Alam Kehidupan dan Manunggaling dalam Serat Jatimurti', *ATAVISME*, 16(2).

Baltes, G., 2018, 'The Prodigal Son and His Angry Brother: Jacob and Esau in a Parable of Jesus?', in L. Bornmann (ed.), *Abraham's Family: a Network of Meaning in Judaism, Christianity, and Islam*, pp. 275–290, Mohr Siebeck Tubingen, Tubingen.

Barbato, M., 2016, 'What kind of person is the state? the pilgrim as a processual metaphor beyond the Leviathan oa', *Journal of International Relations and Development*, 19(4).

Burke, T., 2013, 'The parable of the prodigal father: An interpretative key to the third gospel', *Tyndale Bulletin*.

Clark-King, E., 2007, 'The Prodigal son (Luke 15:11–32)', *The Expository Times*, 118(5), 238–239.

Culpepper, A., 1995, 'The Gospel of Luke', in L. Kick (ed.), *The New Interpreter's Bible Vol. IX*, pp. 3–490, Abingdon, Nashville, Tennessee.

Delcorno, P., 2017, *In the Mirror of the Prodigal son: The Pastoral Uses of a Biblical Narrative (c. 1200–1550)*, Brill, Leiden, the Netherlands.

Endraswara, S., 2006, *Mistik Kejawen: sinkretisme, simbolisme, dan Sufisme dalam budaya Spiritual Jawa*, 1st edn., Narasi, Yogyakarta.

Evans, V. & Green, M., 2006, *Cognitive linguistics: An introduction*.

Fan, H., 2017, 'A Study of "Hand" Metaphors in English and Chinese—Cognitive and Cultural Perspective', *Advances in Literary Study*.

Fitzmyer, J.A., 1981, *The Gospel according to Luke : introduction, translation, and notes*, Doubleday, Garden City, N.Y. :

Hultgren & J., A., 2000, *The Parable of Jesus: A Commentary*, Eerdmans, WB,

Grand Rapids: Eerdmans.

Jack, A., 2019, *The Prodigal Son in English and American Literature*, Oxford University Press, Oxford, UK.

Kasnadi, K. & Sutejo, 2018, 'Islamic Religious Values within Javanese Traditional Idoms as the Javanese Life Guidlelines', *El Harakah*, 20(1), 33–48.

Keller, T., 2008, *The Prodigal God: Recovering the Heart of Christian Faith*, Hodder & Stoughton, London, UK.

Klyne Snodgrass, 2018, *Stories with Intent: A Comprehensive Guide to the Parable of Jesus*, 2nd ed., Grand Rapids, Eerdmans.

Kratz, E.U., 1985, 'Nikolaus Girardet [and] Susan Piper and R. M. Soetanto: Descriptive catalogue of the Javanese manuscripts and printed books in the main libraries of Surakarta Yokyakarta. (Schriftenreihe des Südasien-Instituts [Heidelberg], 30.) xx, 1128 pp. Wiesbaden: Fr', *Bulletin of the School of Oriental and African Studies*.

Linnemann, E., 1986, *Jesus of the Parables: Introduction and Exposition*, 1st ed., SPCK, London, UK.

Naseri, C., 2017, 'Reading Luke 15:11-32 as the Parable of Mercy and Compassion, *Caban*, 9, 142–159.

Nauta, R., 2008, 'The Prodigal Son: Some Psychological Aspects of Augustine's Conversion to Christianity', *Journal of Religion and Health*, 47(1), 75–87.

Onisim, L.A., 2017, 'The Parable of the Prodigal Son: A Cognitive Linguistic Analysis', *Centrul de Studii Biblico-Filologice Monumenta Linguae Dacoromanorum*, 7(1), 135–149.

Pigeaud, T., 1967, *Literature of Java.*, Martinus Nyjhoff, De Hague.

Prawiroadmojo, 1989, *Bausastra Jawa-Indonesia*, Gunung Agung, Jakarta.

Siswanto, J., 2016, 'Metafisika Serat Jatimurti', *Jurnal Filsafat*, 20(1), 1–25.

Soedjonoredjo, 1980, *Serat jatimurti*, transl. Anomim, 2nd edn., UP Yayasan Djojobojo, Surabaya.

Soemotjitro & Jendral, K.D., 1980, 'Paguyuban Warga Hardo Pusoro: Panuntun Kawruh Hardo Pusoro', Proyek Inventarisasi Kepercayaan terhadap Tuhan Yang Maha Esa (Indonesia). (Inventarization Project -The Indigenous Beliefs in Indonesia), 1st edn., Departemen Pendidikan dan Kebudayaan (Ministry of Education and Culture), Jakarta.

Susanto, H., 2020, 'Panggilan Sosial Gereja Berdasarkan Pelayanan Jesus dalam Lukas 4:18-19: Sebuah Upaya Merevitalisasi Pelayanan Gereja', *Veritas*, 19(1), 99–101.

Sweetman, B., 2012, 'Homo Viator: Introduction to the Metaphysic of Hope. By Gabriel Marcel. Translated by Emma Craufurd and Paul Seaton.', American Catholic Philosophical Quarterly.
Vos, C., 2014, 'Homo Viator, Verbum et Ecclesia.
Young, B.H., 2008, The Parables: The Jewish Tradition and Christian Interpretation, Baker Publishing Group, Grand Rapids, MI.

This article has been published in ***Varitas: Theology and Ministry Journal*, 20 no. 1. (2021):107-124.**
Perjalanan Spiritual Homo Viator: Studi Komparatif Serat Jatimurti dengan Perumpamaan tentang Anak yang Hilang (Luk. 15: 11–32) **(The Journey of Homo Viator: Comparative Study of Serat Jatimurti and The Parable of the Prodigal Son (Luke 15:11-15)**
pISSN: 1411-7649; eISSN: 2684-9194 DOI: https://doi.org/10.36421/veritas.v20i1.465, July 8, 2021.

The Meaning of Love in Yunus Emre and Jacopone da Todi's Works

Abstract

Two mystics of the 13th century, Yunus Emre, a Turkish Sufi, and Jacopone da Todi, an Italian Franciscan friar wrote poems that consist of "love" as the most frequently appearing term. There have been many studies done on each of their works, but none compares their views of mystical love, especially concerning mystical union, a theme that occurs frequently with the term "love." This study explores the question of whether their views of love have more similarities or differences by comparing the aspects of love, the centre of love and its origin, and the end of the journey in love. Through thematic analysis, the results show that both conveyed a similar view about love, its origin, and the union with God as the destination of love. However, although they similarly view love as centred on God, their views of God show differences. Jacopone focuses on Christ as God who embraces pain and suffering in expressing the "insanity of love," while Yunus is more apophatic in his insight of God. The finding might help the readers to appreciate various spiritual expressions in modern societies and to delve deeper into different insights that might enrich the understanding of their spiritual heritage.

Keywords: Franciscan, *Lauds*, love, mysticism, poems, Sufism

Introduction

Love is one of the most popular themes used in literature, spirituality, or arts. Yet, people define the word "love" by emphasizing its different aspects and thus cause many discourses. Often people relate love to positive emotional expression or sentiment as the opposite of hatred or apathy. Many Greek philosophers distinguish love as familial love, friendly love, romantic love, self-love, and divine love. (Wallace 2019, Part 5) Other philosophers for example, from India or China, might have classified love differently as also the modern scholars. This article compares the understanding of love in the mysticism of Yunus Emre, an Anatolian Sufi with Jacopone da Todi, a Franciscan friar from Umbria, Italy.

Yunus Emre gains wide recognition in Turkish Sufi circles as they recite or sing hundreds of his poems in the 13th century and afterwards. Today, there is a celebration to honour him on May 25 when people visit his tomb in the corner of Anatolia, Turkey. Comparatively, Jacopone's Laud is referred to among the Franciscan communities every September 15 each year. Today, his works receive recognition beyond the Franciscan Orders or scholars.

Both Yunus Emre (hence: Yunus) and Jacopone da Todi (hence: Jacopone) communicate their insight into spiritual or love journeys in the form of poems. Through such expressions, they hint that God is the initiator of humans' capability to experience love and give love in return. Some scholars in the past point out that Yunus views God as a pantheistic concept and Jacopone's view of God is influenced by his view on Mary's experience as the Mother of Jesus. This study shows that both findings might need corrections.

The works of Yunus Emre as a Sufi mystic receive recognition among the English and German-speaking scholars only after the publication of Mehmed Fuat Koprülu's in 1918 entitled *the First Mystics in Turkish Literature* (Köprülü, Leiser, and Dankoff 2006). Furthermore, substantial studies emerge following the works of Abdülbaki Gölpınarlı, a Turkish historian (Gölpınarlı 1961). Thus, in modern Turkey today, when the nation rediscovers and reevaluates the wealth or their inherited literature, people begin to realize the significance of Yunus Emre's poems. His thoughts and words appear in various media, from novels to daily columns, or even political discussions. A television serial about Yunus Emre, *Journey to the Beloved* spreads internationally in 2019.

Jacopone's background is coloured by his wealthy and respected family in Umbria, Northern Italy. After completing his education, he occupies a prominent position in the legal world. Later, Jacopone da Todi becomes a lay brother of the Spiritual Order of Franciscans. As a lay member of the Order, Jacopone writes more than one hundred forty Lauds that are still popular today.

Interestingly, despite the different social contexts and faith of Yunus Emre, a Muslim, and Jacopone da Todi, a Catholic, those two mystics of the 13th century use similar terms or expressions related to love throughout their works. Many questions emerge from the past studies but this article examines the poems of Yunus Emre and the Lauds of Jacopone da Todi to answer several questions that centre around love: does the term love in both poems mean the same or is there a significant difference? Is love mainly a human intense emotion? Where does love originate? Who is the centre of love? What is the end of the love in their spiritual journey?

The Methodology
This study is qualitative. Through the thematic analysis of the poems of Yunus Emre (hence: Yunus) and the Lauds of Jacopone da Todi (hence: Jacopone) the method, this article tries to uncover the meaning of love by analyzing its relationship with several terms that repeatedly appears in both works when those mystics share their insight about love. Few metaphors that relate to love will also receive special attention. Therefore, a brief description of each of the mystic poets' social or cultural contexts will be given to give a proper understanding of the terms and metaphors.

To do so, several steps will be taken. First, the article lists some well-known stanzas that consist of love and related terms. Second, the terms that each mystic uses to explain the term "love" will be identified to uncover how each term represents an aspect of love. Third, the study categorizes the terms to uncover the aspects of love that the mystics emphasize. In both steps, allegories, metaphors, or non-linear expressions that they use to describe "love" also receive serious analyses. Then, the study proposes the relationship of those categories to understand the richness or the embedded meanings or to identify the most salient "constellations" of meanings in gaining the proper insight on "love" related to the questions of the study.

The thematic analysis might have risks. First, the richness of the terms that the mystics use to share their insights of love might cause the study to focus only on a few popular terms that past studies have analyzed in each mystic while neglecting other less-known terms. Another risk is the study might overlook unique terms that have not been studied until today. To prevent such shortcomings, the study explores as many as possible the available poems and Lauds.

The purpose of this study is to contribute insights for further comparative spirituality research. Readers who live in a religiously pluralistic nation where various spirituality types live and try to give answers to people's quest for love, the meaning of life, or its destination can benefit from the findings. For some people who might stereotype the Islamic faith as more centred on law, the theme of love in Sufism might enrich their understanding of various spectrums in Islam spirituality. Those, who might generalize that most Catholic mystics tend to exclude emotions in their spiritual expression, might learn that authentic passion and emotional, or romantic expressions related to God's love have also a place in their spiritual journey. (Başkal 2010) Those purposes do not mean to promote religious relativism but more into developing a deeper mutual appreciation.

As a limitation, the article does not delve too much into the meaning of the terms "death" and "journey" in the poems and Lauda as those terms lie outside the main focus of this study. Also, following many past studies in English, this work relies mainly on the English translations of Yunus Emre's works done by Dilaver (2021), Ahmad Sezer (1967), Başkal (Başkal 2010) and Faiz (Faiz 1992) with the works of Gölpınarli (Gölpınarlı 1961) and Mustafa Tatçi ((Tatçi 1990) as their references. Concerning the source of Jacopone da Todi's works, the classical translation of Jacopone's Lauds by Theodore Beck in Evelyn Underhill's work (Underhill 1919) serves as the main source together with the translation of Elizabeth Hughes and Serge Hughes. (Hughes and Hughes 1982)

Result

1. Poems as the Object of the Study
In general, poetic communication was a part of the oral culture. Relating poems to all languages of transcendent, no matter how different from each other, they tend to express embedded views or teachings by using a similar grammar and vocabulary to produce "a sacred rhetoric" (Franceschini 2012, 19). In the case of

poetry, the similarities are not only semiotic but also ontological. Many are insights related to common steps of: "Experience of the void, death of the ego, an explosion of the heart" (Plouvier 2002, 11). To understand the meanings of the love of Yunus and Jacopone in their poems, the study needs to describe poems and Lauds mainly their functions in the 13th-century contexts and the reason that the mystics use such art forms.

In the most scholarly edition of Yunus' works edited by Mustafa Tatçi, there are approximately 415 poems, including his long didactic poem or advice called *Risalatu'n Nushiyya* (Tatçi 2012). Yunus writes in vernacular Turkish with musical accompaniment. The function of his poems is to describe the experiences and struggles of human beings on their journey to God. The dominant voice of the poems is about love and life destination in the union of God's love.

The development of Christian mysticism is deeply bound to poetics. Jacopone is not the first Christian mystic who uses poems or Lauds (incantation poems) to share his insight.

Concerning the characteristics of Jacopone and his works, various scholars have different views. Novati mentions that Jacopone is a theoretical mystic as shown in his Lauds (Novati 1908). D'Ancona (D'Ancona 1914) states that Jacopone is a minstrel of God which means that he colours his Lauds with simplicity as he follows the path of Saint Francis Later, Mario Casella points out that Jacopone was a pure mystic and represents the rebellious voice of the Franciscan (Casella 1920, 281–339). Interestingly, in 1961, de Sanctis categorizes Jacopone as an illiterate and ignorant friar with profane poetry, theology, and philosophy (De Sanctis 1961).

As Giles Meerssemann states, from the beginning of the thirteenth century, any religious lyric poem in the vernacular was called a *Lauda* (Meerssemann 1962). The early *Lauda* was probably influenced by the music of the troubadours since it showed similarities in rhythm, melodic style, and especially notation. The *Lauda* or Lauds spread widely throughout Europe during the 13th and 14th centuries and picked up the vernacular language in each country where it was accepted. Merriam-Webster Dictionary points out that Troubadour is one of a class of lyric poets and poet-musicians often of knightly rank who flourishes from the 11th to the end of the 13th century chiefly in the south of France and the north of Italy and whose major theme is courtly love ("Troubadour" 2021).

Therefore, both mystics use poems and Lauds as they have two objectives. First, respectively they live in Turkey and Italy which at that historical stage maintained the orality or the oral culture. With those art forms, Yunus and Jacopone could connect heart-to-heart with their people, especially since they choose to use vernacular language in poems and Lauds. Such choices indicate their reluctance to reach only the high-class members of the society or the choices might show their unwillingness to classify people based on hierarchy, a normal framework at that time. Thus, as Dilaver summarizes Yunus speaks to everyone in every segment of the society including the high-class or the intellectuals (Dilaver 2021, 37). Second, the poems or Lauds are not meant to fulfil the artistic preferences of both mystics. Deliberately Yunus uses poems as a form to share his insight and experience. Written in one of his poems is a sentence *Yunus Hak tecellisin siir dilinden soyler* (Gölpınarlı, Abdülbâkî 1943, 129) which means Yunus speaks of the Truth's manifestation through the language of poetry. The forms also serve as a way to bring people to the awareness of humans' language limitations as each of the mystics repeatedly state in their works. Both of them indicate that love or God's love could not be described completely by using ordinary language. Such a concept is evident in one of the stanzas of Yunus' poems: "*Suddenly did I see a face; no word was with it. Were I to say its secret, impossible, in a language it cannot be contained*" (Gölpınarlı, Abdülbâkî 1943, 79). Furthermore, to achieve the second objective they also use paradox or contradictory words in their expressions to strengthen their message.

2. Analysis of the Characteristics of Love

Love is the most frequent word that appears in Yunus' and Jacopone's works. Numerous poems and Lauds consist of the word alongside other terms or metaphors. This section analyses the relationship between them and uncovers the aspects of love and the meanings that each mystic conveys in their works.

a. Love in Yunus' Poems

The word love as a noun in Turkey is **"aşk" which appears in most of Yunus' poems.** The word can also mean, passion, crush, amour, gallantry, or adoration. For example, Yunus writes his most well-known stanza "*Aşkın aldı benden beni*" or in English "your love has taken me away from myself." Although Sezer states that the real stanza should be "*Işkun aldi benden beni*" or, "*Thy love has taken me away from me.*" (Sezer 1967, 82), fundamentally both translations do not show any significant difference in the meaning. In the poem, the phrase "taken away" can also be translated as "wrested away" which has the same meaning. The term love in this poem shows that love is something that has the emotional capability or power to make a person experience its intensity.

The phrase does not stand alone as in another poem, there is a similar expression "your love took me away and made me forget about myself..." which is continued with "Let me burn upon drinking the wine of love by losing myself in the words and eyes of the true friend." (Dilaver 2021, 173). Several other poems mention that "love of his Creator intoxicated him," (Dilaver 2021, 289) or "look well, where a lover is there, too beloved will be in ecstasy…" (Faiz 1992, 33) All those stanzas indicate another characteristic of love that Yunus describes: Love is something that intoxicates a person. A person in love might no longer be able to control him- or herself.

Another characteristic of love can be uncovered in the following stanzas in various Yunus' poems,

Your love makes the lovers abandon all the wealth and desires,
detaches the lovers from their own selves, and makes them die before death.
(Dilaver 2021, 173).

l abandoned all my wishes and desire
(Dilaver 2021, 181).

If I am really in love with you, I should not be afraid of reproach.
I should be able to sacrifice my soul with pleasure.
(Köprülü, Leiser, and Dankoff 2006).

If you live within love, should sacrifice your life for love,
you should consume your life for love.
(Dilaver 2021, 165).

If I am really in love with you, I should not be afraid of reproach.
I should be able to sacrifice my soul with pleasure.
(Başgöz 2020, 225)

The love that clings to soul this is not any Love;
Who casts not soul aside sees not the Loved One's Face.
(Faiz 1992, 27)

Thus, all those stanzas in various poems point out that for Yunus, love relates to abandonment and sacrifice.

Yunus also expresses another feeling related to love "I have lost my mind ever since I loved you… I lost myself in the Truth by reaching the sea like the rivers." … I fell into the fire of love, and yearned and burned." Similar occurrence of the word "burned" or fire" is also in one of his poems "Whoever has love has nothing left in him… " (Dilaver 2021, 195) or in a phrase "My body burns with love like a fire bush…" (Dilaver 2021, 199) lastly, in one of his poems, "the fire of you love tears my heart out; I burn with your love, and this burning pleases me." (Dilaver 2021, 255). In one of the poems, Yunus even gives a strong expression, "I forgot everything, religion and piety got past me with love, what kind of a sect this love is, it is even deeper than the religion." (Dilaver 2021, 143). Those poems as examples of many others show that for Yunus, love is something that burns or annihilates and brings nothingness, but also brings happiness or pleasure.

Thus far, for Yunus, the word "love" occurs together frequently with the following terms, abandonment, intoxication, losing selfhood, forget me, annihilation, nothingness, or being burned in love even in his many other poems.

Table 1: Love and the Categories of its Aspects According to Yunus

Love in Yunus' poems		
Phrases in Yunus' poems	Terms related to Love	Category
Your love has taken me away from myself, Let me burn upon drinking the wine of love by losing myself	Intoxication	The emotional power or intensity of love
Your love makes the lovers abandon all the wealth and desires, detaches the lovers from their own selves	Abandonment and sacrifice	
I fell into the fire of love and yearned and burned	Loss of selfhood and annihilation	The Consequences of Love
I burn with your love, and this burning pleases me	Happiness	

The conclusion thus far is that love has an intensity or power beyond a person's capability to control it. Instead, love can control the person. A question emerges, "is it logical that if love is merely an emotional state as such, it will be able to drive a person to enter nothingness or to abandon selfhood for the sake of love itself?

b. Love in Jacopone's Lauds

In Jacopone's Lauds, many times the term "love" appears. In Laud 67, Jacopone shares his experience with love.

> Tell me, Love, why have You left me in grief and uncertainty?
> Is it my vileness that repels You? Let me make amends.
> If I reshape myself, will You not come back?
> Love, why did You give my heart such sweetness,
> Only to strip it then of joy?
> *(Hughes and Hughes 1982, 264)*

In that Laud, Jacopone describes his experience that love relates to sweetness but also grief. Furthermore, love brings confusion. In that Lauds, he poses an unanswerable question, an expression that can be found in other Jacopone's poems.

In Lauds 79 one of the stanzas expresses it as follows

> Infinite love demands again,
> It claims the soul, the heart, the brain,
> All time, all being, for its own.
> It asks a patient, faithful love,
> Enduring through Eternity
> A love instinct with highest hopes,
> Beyond Heaven's utmost mystery:
> A love embracing everything,
> And generous in charity,
> That on the heart's humility
> Hath built her dwelling and her throne.
> *(Underhill 1919, 451)*

The poem shows that love embraces the soul, heart, and brain. Love is also infinite but it can dwell in one's heart that has humility in it. More than questioning, Jacopone admits that he experiences confusion caused by love as expressed in Laud 89. *"Suddenly bereft of You, I know not where I am; Confused, I look for You all about."* (Hughes and Hughes 1982, 205)

Love also teaches a person who is in love to change as expressed in Laud 90, "For this Love, I have renounced all/traded the world and myself" (Hughes and Hughes 1982, 257) and also in Laud 91.

> The soul by Love is taught
> All his beliefs and his thought
> Were foolish and poor and blind,
> Tumult and tempest and wind,
> Error and falsity.
> *(Underhill 1919, 491)*

The changes in a person's thoughts and beliefs mean that love transforms a person to the point that he or she recognizes his or her foolishness and shortcoming. The person even wishes to abandon the world or selfhood.

His most popular Laud 90 which has more than 25 stanzas explains more about his struggles.

> Love, that art Charity,
> Why hast Thou hurt me so?
> Before I knew its power,
> I asked in prayer
> For love of Christ, believing it was sweet
> I thought to breathe a calm and tranquil air,
> On peaceful heights, Where tempests never beat.
> Torment I find, instead of sweetness there!
> My heart is riven by the dreadful heat
> Of these strange things to treat
> All words are vain;
> By bliss, I am slain,
> And yet I live and move.
> *(Underhill 1919, 380).*

For Jacopone as he expresses again in Laud 90, first, love is a powerful emotional state that includes intense pain and struggles instead of the sweetness that he has expected. Yet, he continues moving on. Second, in the fourth stanza of the Laud, he continues sharing his experience that a person who has no power to resist love.

> For this Love, I have renounced all,
> Traded the world and myself;
> Were I the lord of creation
> I would give it all away for Love.
> And yet Love still plays with me,
> Makes me act as if out of my senses,
> Destroys me and draws me I know not where—
> But since I sold myself I have no power to resist.
> *(Underhill 1919, 381)*

The presence of love in his heart also causes his willingness to abandon many things including the world and himself. Thus, love and abandonment are closely related.

Observing Laud 90, many more are written, "Love has captured me and I know not where I am or what I am doing or saying." Then, "Crying out its love, The soul drowns in ecstasy!" Further, it also consists of the following stanza, "Love that consumes and binds me tight! Sweet Love, consider my suffering I cannot endure the fire. Love has captured me and I know not where I am." (Hughes and Hughes 1982, 260) The above-listed stanzas express Jacopone's experience and insight that love is not only powerful but also intoxicates him. However, again, he expresses the uncertainty of the direction that love brings him into.

Table 2: Love and the Categories of Its Aspects According to Jacopone

Love in Jacopone's Lauds		
Phrases	Terms related to Love	Category
Infinite love demands again, It claims the soul, the heart, the brain,	Love demands, Claim the Soul, the heart, the brain	Love influences human life totally
A love embracing everything	Love embraces	

	Everything	
Tell me, Love, why have You left me in grief and uncertainty?	Pain, Uncertainty	Love brings uncertainty
The soul by Love is taught All his beliefs and his thought Were foolish and poor and blind, Tumult and tempest and wind, Error and falsity.	Taught foolishness	Love teaches a person
Love, why did You give my heart such sweetness, only to strip it then of joy?	Why Sweetness Joy	Love brings along question and confusion
Love, that art Charity, Why hast Thou hurt me so?	Hurt	
Suddenly bereft of You, I know not where I am; Confused, I look for You all about."	Confused	
For this Love I have renounced all, Traded the world and myself;	Renounced Traded	Love causes the lover to abandon many things
And yet Love still plays with me, makes me act as if out of my senses	Plays Out of my senses	Love causes intoxication
But since I sold myself I have no power to resist.	Power Resist	The emotional power or intensity of love
For this Love, I have renounced all	Abandonment and sacrifice	Love causes the lover to abandon many things
Makes me act as if out of my senses,	Out of my senses	Love causes Intoxication
Destroys me and draws me I know not where—	Loss of self-hood	Love brings uncertainty

From the exploration of those Lauds, it is evident as has been stated before that for Jacopone love is something that has tremendous intensity and power. The impact of love is on the total life of a person who is in love. Among others, love is something that causes the abandonment of one's selfhood. In Jacopone's personal life, it is evident that after he became a wandering monk, he was accepted in the Franciscan convent and accepted unfair treatment from his fellow friars. (Underhill 1919, 75) More than that, love is something that brings also pain and joy, sweetness and bitterness or confusion. Then, love is something that entails uncertainty for a person who is in love. Yet, love can drive a person to renounce the world and self-hood. Many more Lauds of Jacopone echo the same themes as if he shouts to heaven.

Thus far, to compare the results of the exploration of the aspects of love in Yunus Emre and Jacopone's work in this step, the following table will be used

Table 3: Comparison between Yunus' and Jacopone's Insights about Love

Comparison between Love in Yunus' and Jacopone's works		
The Terms related to love		The Category
Yunus Emre	Jacopone	
Intoxication	Intoxication	Emotional Power and intensity of love
Abandonment and sacrifice	Abandonment and sacrifice	
Loss of Selfhood	Loss of Selfhood	The consequences of love
	Uncertainty	

The table shows that for both mystics, love is a very powerful emotional state that very powerful. One whose heart is filled with love will have a willingness to bear all consequences of living with love. Abandonment, confusion, sweetness, joy, pain, sacrifice, or even loss of self-hood are some of the many more consequences of love.

After concluding that for Yunus and Jacopone love has an emotional intensity or power and brings many consequences, at least three questions arise. Why does love possess so much power? Where does love originate? Also, another question logically emerges: who or what is the centre of such a powerful love? To answer the questions, the study explores more stanzas and poems of Yunus and Jacopone's lauds.

c. The Center and Origin of Love in Yunus' Poems
The term "love" in the above-mentioned poems might indicate the poet's love for a human being. For example, in one stanza, Yunus writes "*I love you will all my*

heart." (Dilaver 2021, 143) Yunus even adds more "*I cannot reach Him.*" (Dilaver 2021, 143) In another poem it is written, "*I Love You With All My Heart.*" In some poems, the term "Beloved" appears such as *"Once you have loved the One Beloved, no more may sorrow size your host."* (Faiz 1992, 105) Also, there are phrases similar to this sentence, *"Just like is visible everywhere on every being with its colours, you are also visible in every being wherever I look; you are everywhere."* What do the terms "You, Him, or the Beloved" mean? Does he direct his love to another human being?

The question can be answered by the following stanzas of various poems by Yunus.

> Those who get to know Your Love will become the best of the best.
> My essence could not get enough of Your love.
> *(Dilaver 2021, 149).*

> The Friend from sorrow brought to us His joy; I offer it to all, In outward form, a man - within I am a soul and a beloved.
> *(Faiz 1992, 61).*

> Who, in the pre-Creation feast of friends the Face of Friendship saw, He is the Lover's soul: of Him, you may seek tidings of His Love.
> *(Faiz 1992, 72)*

> God, give me such a love that I forget about myself; such a love myself lose
> *(Dilaver 2021, 249)*

> God has given and will give love to the one whom he says mine So the one who has a bit of love Has also had the existence of God
> *(Küçük and Aslan 2008, 15–16)*

Those poems indicate that the words "love" appear together with the terms "Your Love", "the Friend", "His", and "God." Further occurrences of the words "Friends, Master, or Truth" together with "love" indicate that Yunus understands love as Divine love, not merely human intense emotion or affection between human beings.

The stanza in "My Love for the Creator" supports the conclusion as it describes "the love for my Creator fell into my heart and made a wound in my heart" and then continues with "My Creator showed his divine light to me and pleased me… He made my heart his throne." (Dilaver 2021, 289)

Furthermore, two of his poems consist of terms like eternal, predestines, and creation.

> The lover assumes that he lives what he desires to;
> but even that desire comes with a state,
> the Almighty One determines and predestines the states of all of us…..
> God predestines those experienced with love.
> All the states of the lovers are predestined by the Beloved.
> *(Dila*ver 2021, 175)

> Who, in the pre-Creation feast of friends the Face of Friendship saw,
> His is the Lover's soul: of him, you may seek tidings of His Love.
> While yet nor earth nor sky had been created Love in Being was;
> For Love eternal is - whatever is of you was born of Love
> *(Faiz 1992, 72)*

In those stanzas, there is another aspect of love that Yunus emphasizes. The poem signifies the role of God as the Almighty who predestines and initiates love to be experienced by human beings. God is the One who initiates love for human beings. Thus, someone can experience or have love in the soul because love originates from the Almighty who wants to give it to human beings.

Furthermore, love is something given by God to those who want it by helping the person remove the ego as written in the following stanza, *"Yunus now speak so that God became the cupbearer to offer you wine, eras the doubt in your heart."* (Dilaver 2021, 154). A similar description of God's role to allow humans to experience love is in the following poem,

> God! Give me such a love that I forget about myself;
> such a love that I lose myself,
> such that I do not find myself even I want
> .… take me and remove this ego from me and fill me with you.
> *(Dilaver 2021, 249)*

What is God's intention in doing so? Yunus gives his insight to answer the question in one of his poems,

> Our Almighty Creator wanted to be known
> by exhibiting His names and attributes
> through all the creatures in such an enormous universe....
> He created the plurality of the realm of creation
> out of the oneness of His essence ...
> *(Dilaver 2021, 46).*

The Almighty does not only create love to be experienced but also enables human beings to experience such love. The experience is related to a person's understanding of the meaning of life and that everything and everyone is created out of the oneness of God's essence. Such understanding also appears in Yunus' other poem "You already know, everyone will come to pass; you already know, no one stays here forever, those who understand the true meaning of this will drink the juice of love." (Dilaver 2021, 157) The word "meaning" and "juice of love" indicates that to experience love, as a prerequisite a person should learn to understand the true meaning of life. Thus, God enables human beings to find the meaning of their existence that God wants humans to come to an understanding of oneness with the Creator.

Yunus' view of the meaning of life can be found in other poems. In one of his poems, he states "One should grasp love and never let it go in order not to be deprived at the end of this life. If you learn one letter of love, if you know the first letter of love that is 'alif', then you do not need to ask any questions to anyone. (Dilaver 2021, 165) The word 'alif' in the alphabet is the first one as in the term "aşk" or love. The sentence shows that love exists as the first among other things during the process of creation. Relating the word to the term "life", then means that at the beginning of life, love already exists as God creates such. Love also exists until the end of life. With such understanding, one is ready to enter the journey of love as the gift of God. To support such a conclusion another stanza can receive special attention: *"Love is not of human mother born, and is a slave to none, But every friend and every enemy is subject to Love's rule."* (Faiz 1992, 98)

To sum up, Yunus shares his insight that love exists since the beginning of time. God is the creator of love. God's essence also exists in human beings and other creations. As God's essence presents in a person, once the person realizes it and understands the meaning of life and the experience of Divine love is possible as God enables the person to walk in a journey or process to love God. The ability to do so is embedded in humans' essence as God designed as such, as the Almighty wants to be known and loved by human beings. The following table summarizes the centre and origin of love according to Yunus as written in his many poems.

Table 4: The Center and Origin of Love According to Yunus

The Center and Origin of Love According to Yunus		
Phrase	Terms related to love	Category
If you learn one letter of love, if you know the first letter of love that is 'alif'	First	Where love begins
God! Give me such a love	God gives Love	God is the creator of love
God predestines those experienced with love	God predestines	
Those who understand the true meaning of this will drink the juice of love	The true meaning of life	

d. The Center and Origin of Love in Jacopone's Lauds

Compared to Yunus' poem, who is the centre of love as described in the works of Jacopone? Where does love originate?

In Lauds 80, Jacopone speaks about love as if he has a dialogue with someone,

> Do you know of the Love that has swept me up
> And continues to hold my heart,
> That keeps me imprisoned in its sweetness—
> The Love that would have me die in pain?

The reply is much in the same melodious vein:

> The love about which you inquire
> We know in many forms;

> Yet if you do not speak of your beloved
> We know not how to answer you.
> *(Hughes and Hughes 1982, 35)*

Thus, the poem points out that love is centred on "the beloved" not on oneself or the person who is in love. Then, the self-hood of the person can become a hindrance to genuine love. Furthermore, in Lauds 83, there is a unique verse

> O sweet Love, You who have killed Your Beloved,
> I beg of You, let me die of Love!
> Love, You who led Your Lover
> To such a hard death, why have You done this?
> Was it that You did not want me to perish?
> Do not spare me, let me die in Love's embrace.
> You did not spare Him whom You loved so dearly;
> Why then be indulgent with me?
> *(Hughes and Hughes 1982, 240)*

The stanza has a verse that might provide an answer to the earlier question about Jacopone's subject or object of love. The verse is "You did not spare Him whom You loved so dearly." Who is the One that Jacopone speaks about? In the poem, the verse has a continuation in the following "*Love is fixed to the cross—The cross has taken Him and will not let Him go. I run and cling to that cross.*" (Hughes and Hughes 1982, 241) Thus, for Jacopone, Jesus Christ is the centre of his love.

What is the origin of such love? In Laud 89, "*Un arbore e da Dio plantato*" (the Tree of Divine Love), Jacopone also creates the following stanza

> There is a tree planted by God which we call Love.
> You there, you I see up in its branches—
> Show me where I can begin to climb,
> That I might leave this darkness behind.
> I climb so slowly that if I stop to speak to you
> A puff of wind will blow me down.
> I have a long way to go;
> Indeed, there's a hard struggle ahead.
> *(Hughes and Hughes 1982, 253–55)*

In that stanza, love is planted by God. Thus, God is the creator of love and enables people to journey in love, a process that he explains by using the metaphor of climbing a tree.

Lauds 83 might shed light on the question that has been posed before concerning the centre of love:

> O, gentle Love,
> Who died for Love,
> I pray Thee,
> Slay me for Love!
> Love, Who didst lead
> To death indeed,
> Thy Lover upon the Cross,
> 0 tell me why
> Thy Dear must die?
> —' Twas to redeem my loss.
> *(Underhill 1919, 287)*

The meaning is clear. The word love that Jacopone refers to is the love of God. Love is then something directed or centred on the person who loves but on God.

It is more apparent in the stanzas of one of Jacopone's last lauds.

> Love, Love-Jesus, I have reached the port,
> Love, Love-Jesus, you have brought me here,
> Love, Love-Jesus, comfort me,
> Love, Love-Jesus, you have enflamed me so much,
> Love, Love-Jesus, consider my needs,
> Allow me to stay, love, in your embrace,
> With thee transformed in true charity,
> In the supreme truth of transformed love.
> (Jacopone, *Laude*, 89.251–8; Mancini 1990: 326–7)

The lauds signify that for Jacopone, God initiates his journey as expressed in Lauds 98

> O, why didst Thou create me,
> Great God of Heaven above
> Redeem me, and await me,
> Through Jesus Christ my Love?
> Thou, Love, didst give me life,
> In tender graciousness
> But guilt in me was rife,
> So great my foolishness
> In misery and strife,
> I roamed the wilderness,
> Till Mary bent to bless,
> And turned me to my Love.
> *(Underhill 1919, 315)*

Furthermore, Jacopone's love centres on the love of Jesus who brought him to God. The love of God is unique and for Jacopone, it is insanity that God loves people so intensely and sacrifices as much as he expressed in Laud 73.

> For since God's wisdom, though so great,
> In all intoxicate with love,
> Shall mine not be inebriate?
> And so be like my Lord above?
> No greater honour can I prove
> Then sharing His insanity.
> (Lauda LXXIII " O derrata, guarda al prezo.") (Underhill 1919, 79)

Table 5: The Center and Origin of Love According to Jacopone

The Center and Origin of Love According to Jacopone		
Phrase	Terms related to Love	Category
The love about which you inquire, We know in many forms;	Many forms	Love manifests itself in many forms

Yet if you do not speak of your beloved, We know not how to answer you.	You beloved	Love is directed to or centred on the beloved.
O sweet Love, You who have killed Your Beloved, I beg of You, let me die of Love! Love, You who led Your Lover, To such a hard death, why have You done this?	Love .. killed Your Beloved, Led Your Lover, Hard death	Love is centred on Jesus and His death on the Cross
Love is fixed to the cross—The cross has taken Him and will not let Him go. I run and cling to that cross	The cross HIm	
O, gentle Love, Who died for Love, I pray Thee, Slay me for Love! Love, Who didst lead]To death indeed, Thy Lover upon the Cross, 0 tell me why Thy Dear must die?	Died for Love, Thy Lover upon the Cross	
There is a tree planted by God which we call Love.	Planted by God	Love is originated in God
The soul wills and yet does not will: Its will belongs to Another	Belong to	Love is centred on God
Love, Love-Jesus, consider my needs, Allow me to stay, love, in your embrace	God's embrace	Love is for Jesus, God
No greater honour can I prove than sharing His insanity.	Insanity	Unbelievable quality of God's love

Thus, for both Yunus and Jacopone, love begins with God's love. God enables humans to realize and receive it and then, respond by giving love to God. Yet, for Jacopone, he concludes further that the love of God as God's gift is a unique action of the Almighty. He even calls it insanity, something that for human logic does not make sense. The term insanity is used as Jacopone could not fathom the depth and intensity of such a love that God wishes to sacrifice, endure pains and even death, and allow human beings to enter the Divine union. Thus, love is more than just an emotional state but is related to the essence of God. Table 6 describes the similarities and differences between those two works.

Table 6. Comparison between the Center and Origin of Love in Yunus' and Jacopone's works

Comparison between the Center and Origin of Love in Yunus' and Jacopone's works		
The Terms related to the Center and Origin		The Category
Yunus Emre	Jacopone	
God	God	God as the origin of love
God wants to be known	God is love	
Predestine	Planted by God	
	Christ, Journey, Sharing insanity	God's love in Christ is an insanity
Journey, after knowing the meaning,		The role of meaning in the love journey

After comparing various aspects of love, those two mystics point out that experiencing love is something that human beings might have as God's gift. However, the receivers should have to undergo a process or journey that is full of struggle until they arrive at the destination. Yunus and Jacopone might have differences in their views concerning the process and the destination as the following analysis will describe.

f. The Process and the Result of Experiencing Divine Love in Yunus' Poem

After a person finds the meaning of life and starts to experience the love that God gives, the process of journeying in love begins. Thus, Yunus viewed that God is the One who initiates or enables humans to journey through such levels of certainties concerning God's calling to love. Gradually, the person changes especially in experiencing certainty as shown in a phrase: *"The lover who sees 'ayn-el yaqïn removes not his eyes from the Friend's face"* (Gölpınarlı, Abdülbâkî 1943, 647–48). The *ayn-el yaqin* which means certainty was also related to *gonul* or heart. Therefore, in short, the process of experiencing love for God gives the person a level of certainty. What will be the end of someone who experiences the love of God?

After the long process, the destination of experiencing love is depicted in many poems by Yunus. In one of the poems, he used metaphors that point out of single identity as the result of the union as he stated that *"just like a drop that falls into the sea and becomes the sea once they unite…"* (Dilaver 2021, 173). Love then means something that unites or merges humans and God.

There is also a stanza that Yunus used to express his feeling "O Friend, my heart and head are one within the furnace of Your Love; But though my heart is in that fire consumed, in that is my delight." (Faiz 1992, 23) The stanza points to the union of human feeling and thinking in God's love.

More Yunus' poems might help to answer the question.

> Look well, where a lover is there too Beloved will be in ecstasy.
> Two in one involved;
> think not that they are two - nor you apart. (*Faiz 1992, 33*)
> I flew aloft from Love's high tower,
> and made its circuit as I passed;
> I was united with the Friend - and sensed no more anxiety.
> I plunged into the oceans' depths;
> the mother-of-pearl in darkness found;
> Myself a gem became; no longer knew the seas' anxiety.
> *(Faiz 1992, 38)*
> As one who serves I looked –
> I looked within myself and saw that
> One Who on this form had life bestowed,
> the One Who is at one with me.
> *(Faiz 1992, 101)*

> The Lord and cup-bearer now one,
> His Love makes drunk all dervish-hood....
> Yunus calls: 'My soul was dead; this Love brought it to life again;
> No more in me is "I" and "You"
> when we shall witness dervish-hood.
> *(Faiz 1992, 114)*

Those stanzas signify that for Yunus, the destination of the journey in love or God's love is a mystical union in God. It might mean that the person's selfhood completely disappears in such a Divine union. The aspects of the union with God can be shown in Table 7.

Table 7: The Process and the Result of Experiencing Divine Love in Yunus' Poem

The Process and the Result of Experiencing Divine Love in Yunus' Poem		
Phrase	Terms related to the Process and the Result	Category
just like a drop that falls into the sea and becomes the sea once they unite	A drop, the sea	Love destination is Immersion
O Friend, my heart and head are one within the furnace of Your Love; But though my heart is in that fire consumed, in that is my delight.	Heart, head, furnace, fire	Love destination is the disappearance of essence
Two in one involved; think not that they are two - nor you apart."	Two, apart	Love means one-ness
I flew aloft from Love's high tower, and made its circuit as I passed; I was united with the Friend.	United	Love is a process to bring someone to Divine union
I looked within myself and saw that One Who on this form had life bestowed, the One Who is at one with me.	At one with me	Love causes recognition of God-human oneness
The Lord and cup-bearer now one, His Love makes drunk all dervish-	No more "I" and "You"	Love brings union and no more two entities.

hood....Yunus calls: 'My soul was dead; this Love brought it to life again; No more in me is "I" and "You"		

g. The Process and the Result of Experiencing Divine Love in Jacopone's Lauds

For Jacopone, the experience of love along the journey brings joy to the end of it as he expressed in the following stanza:

> My madness is the drunkenness of Love –
> all lovers know my state,
> I came to my dual nature to transfigure,
> and to merge with One. *(Rassekh 1987, 50)*

The terms merge or transfigure that relate to the term "love" indicate that love causes immersion or union of the lover and God. Immersion or merging means evaporation of one self-hood as it unites with God's self. Then another Laud clarifies the merging process.

> My heart is fettered fast, it cannot flee;
> It is consumed, like wax set in the sun;
> Living, yet dying, swooning passionately,
> It prays for strength a little way to run,
> Yet in this furnace must it bide and be:
> Where am I led, ah me!
> To depths so high?
> Living I die,
> So fierce the fire of Love *(Mancini 2006, 140).*

In the Lauds as well as in others, Jacopone struggles intensively. His expression signifies that pain and the love of God seemed to be inseparable in the phrase *"living I die, so fierce the fire of love."* The word "fire of love" indicates that love purifies something and the process entails pain as it means a transformation that finally brings annihilation of an entity as expressed in the phrase *"wax set in the sun."*

Another metaphor also points out that love means the human soul immerse in God's

> Just as red-hot iron of forms (air)
> touched by the burning colour of dawn (the sun),
> lose their original contours (to assume another figure),
> so does the soul immersed in You, o love? *(Rassekh 1987, 25)*

Thus, those lauds signify that the end of the journey in love is a total immersion or merge of human essence into God's. It means that at the destination, only a single entity exists.

However, Jacopone also often uses the metaphor of bride and bridegroom as shown in the sentences in his poem: "*And prepare you, the bride of quiet wisdom, to enter the King's chamber and court,*" followed by, "*Come to the gate naked and forlorn,---The robe of a bride approaching her bridegroom.*" (Hughes and Hughes 1982, 132) Furthermore, "*Hurry to embrace your spouse who gathers you into His joy- O love, love.*" (Rassekh 1987, 24) In those metaphors of a joyful wedding, the union of God and humans in love is more like a communion where each entity is maintained.

Table 8:
The Process and the Result of Experiencing Divine Love in Jacopone's Lauds

The Process and the Result of Experiencing Divine Love in Jacopone's Lauds		
Phrase	Terms of the Process and the Result	Category
I came to my dual nature to transfigure, and to merge with One	Transfigure Merge	The destination of love is to merge one entity
It is consumed, like wax set in the sun; Red hot iron forms	Consumed	The destination of Love's journey is annihilation and one entity
So does the soul immersed in You, o Love	Immersed	Destination of love journey is immersion and one entity
Hurry to embrace your spouse who gathers you into His joy- O love, love	Embrace	Destination of love is one-ness but two entities

And prepare you, the bride of quiet wisdom, to enter the King's chamber and court.	Bride	
Come to the gate naked and forlorn, The robe of a bride approaching her bridegroom.	Approaching	

Discusion

There are many similarities between Yunus and Jacopone. Love is the main term that they use and becomes the focus of their insights are evident. They also similarly conclude that life destination is union with God in love. Table 10 maps the similarities and differences in their views.

Table 10. Comparison of the Result of the Journey of Love in Yunus' and Jacopone's works

Comparison of The Result of the Journey Yunus' and Jacopone's works		
The Terms related to the Result of the Journey		The Category
Yunus Emre	Jacopone	
United	United	One entity in the Union with God
Immersion	Immersion	
Melted	Merged	
Consumed	Consumed	
A drop in the sea	Wax set in the sun	
Fire	Red hot iron	
Embraced	Embraced	Two entities in union with God
Layla and Majnun	Spouse, Bride and Bridegroom	
God exists in every creation	God creates everything	Pantheism
God is the Creator	God is love in Christ	God is love, The personhood of the Trinitarian God.

Thus, from the analysis, it is proper to state that Yunus and Jacopone belong to the same type of mysticism or specifically love mysticism, but such categorization is not sufficient to describe the complete dimensions in each teaching of Yunus Emre and Jacopone concerning love.

It is easy to conclude that Yunus seems to emphasize the disappearance of the human entity as it immerses in God while Jacopone seems to depict the union as a romantic or erotic union between a bride and a bridegroom more often as the destination of the love journey. Those who give such a conclusion point out that for Yunus a spiritual journey in love could happen because God gives humans the capability to know and relate to the Creator as God is omnipresent in the universe and expresses the Divine's essence on the plurality including in humans. (Risala quoted by Sezer 1967, 58). The starting point of the journey for Yunus was the awareness of the meaning of life and that God is the One who created the universe and mankind (Sezer 1967, 62) in oneness with God's essence. Then at the end of the journey, humans will unite with God as a water drop enters the sea. However, the conclusion as such concerning Yunus and Jacopone has a risk.

First, based on the past studies on Yunus, compared to many theologians, most mystics show some distinct characteristics in their works related to theology as their views or concepts are based on experiences and emotional or even ecstatic responses. Therefore, their works are like autobiographies, and many expressions are related to their emotionally intense and authentic experience or struggle. Many expressions often contradict each other or become paradoxical to describe God or love.

Second, Yunus also describes the essence of loving intimacy with God parallel with the romantic love that happens between Layla and Majnun (Dilaver 2021, 215) which is similar to Juliet and Romeo. Thus, Yunus might mean that it was not a union in the sense that humanness melted into God's essence. It was more like communion between a bride and bridegroom as he used words such *as asyik* (the lover) and *masyuq* (the beloved). Thus, the union with love or God for Yunus poems as the final spiritual destination can be multi-interpretable.

    a. Concerning God as the centre of love and the journey, the sentence in the poem "through all the creatures in such an enormous universe, He created the plurality of the realm of creation out of the oneness of His essence," might indicate Yunus as a pantheistic mystic. Allesio Bombaci supported such a conclusion as he mentioned that Yunus holds a view that God is present in nature, in human beings, in the past, in the present, and good or evil (Bombaci 1956, 273). Sezer also concluded similarly through his analysis of the concept that Yunus used a term: *wahdat i wujud* which means oneness of beings or unity of existence (Sezer 1967, 61) Thus, the relation between this inner world and God is the most important connection in the whole universe (Başkal 2010, 122). Thus, to connect to God's love, human beings should come to an awareness of God's presence in their heart.

b. Many expressions in his poems indicate that Yunus leans toward a pantheistic view (Sezer 1967, 88) as he uses the concept of *wadhat al wujud*. The term means God presents and exists in every *wujud* (created forms). Therefore, the union means the evaporation of humans' essence as they return to their original essence "just like a drop that falls into the sea and becomes the sea once they unite…" (Dilaver 2021, 173). One of the verses in his poem might explain his views to support the above conclusion: *Bizi is ile fena kil ki nice hest olalum* (annihilate us with love that we are existent) (Gölpınarlı, Abdülbâkî 1943, 191). In the stanza, the first word is *fena* which means nothingness in Turkish. Thus, the sentence means "bring us to nothingness so that we can exist." The second word *hest,* is a term borrowed from Persian that means existent. The paradox is evident. For Yunus, only in love, one's existence becomes non-exist and in such non-existence, one exists. Sezer concluded that Yunus uses a contradiction in his logic that A (which is existence) is not A (which is existence). By doing so, Yunus points out that existence in union with God is completely different from the existence that normal people understand or experience.

c. Such a conclusion is supported by Yunus's further expression in his stanza: *Ne sermayem ola ne var ne yokvem* (I have no capital, neither am I existent nor am I non-existent (Gölpınarlı, Abdülbâkî 1943, 189). In short, Yunus subscribes neither to the communion view nor to the immersion concept of humans and God's union. He was more into a neither-nor logic something that many non-Western religious leaders are familiar with (Nagatomo 2000).

Concerning Jacopone, there are two findings. Coming from a Christian background, Jacopone must be familiar with the thirteenth-century theology that distinguishes two kinds of love: agape and romantic or erotic love. Thus, courtly love becomes the model of men and women's romantic or erotic relations. In keeping with biblical roots, in a theological framework, such romantic or erotic love is regarded as the most fitting metaphor to describe a human-divine love relation. (Greenberg 2016) Jacopone uses the term "super-ardent" love in his most popular poem which shows the dynamic that even a bride-bridegroom relationship does not suffice to describe his personal experience about his relationship with God in Christ. This romantic love brings union as written in verse 99 *"Love makes me go crazy, holds me in His Lordship. In Christ's love, the soul is transformed united in God in all His divinity."* (Zardin n.d., 2) Thus, the union is more like a communion between two lovers.

However, Rassekh states that for Jacopone, in the union with God or God's love, two separate entities melt one another. (Rassekh 1987, 25) as *"just as red-hot iron or forms, touched by the burning colour of the sun lose their contours, so does the soul immerse in You, o Love."* (Franca ed 1953, Lauda XC) There is also a verse in one of the stanzas, *"The soul becomes one with God."*(Hughes and Hughes 1982, 266) Therefore, In short, it is more immersion or melting state rather than a communion of two entities. Thus, according to the Lauds, the human entity disappears in the union.

As Jacopone has strong emotional tones and paradoxical expressions, this study cannot agree with either one of the conclusions of the above studies. Instead, given the artistic language of Lauds, their paradoxical tones, and the uniquely harsh emotional expressions of Jacopone, he might have stated that the union with God is neither communion nor an immersion, but something that humans' words cannot explain. He might even purposely avoid defining the essence of such Divine Union as Jacopone's love as its core could not be understood. A person who is in love with God can only share the sweetness and bliss of such union but cannot completely understand God's insane love for human beings. For Jacopone, his struggles to understand the willingness of God in Christ to do self-sacrifice and endure pains for sinful human beings are more than human words can explain.

In short, both mystics do not indicate that their insights on the union with God lean more on the concept of immersion into a single entity or communion of two entities.

Conclusion

Based on the above explorations and the results, the summary of the similarities and differences related to love as the goal of the study can be listed as follows.

To convey or share their experiences, questions, struggles, and insights,

1. Each of the mystics found a poem or lauds to put into words all their experiences and insights related to love. Love is very powerful. Yet, many times, for both of them the sweetness and pain seemed inseparable from love.
2. Union with God for Yunus Emre and Jacopone da Todi could be similar. The union is neither communion between God's essence and one's identity nor absorption of one's essence or selfhood in the love of God. It means either human identity is annihilated in the union that self-hood disappears, or the identity still exists but is renewed in such union.
3. Concerning God as the centre of love for Yunus, God is the source of love as God gives love to humans. When a human focuses his or her life on love, the person manifests God. Furthermore, in his poems, God takes the initiative to connect God's love to human beings, a fact that makes Yunus call God's love an arrow. Similar to Yunus, for Jacopone, love was given by God. God dwells inside a human's heart that has love at its core. Thus, love was also a guiding force for Jacopone (Rassekh 1987, 14).

Besides the above similarities, the difference between both mystics in their views concerning love also exists. The root of the differences relates to their view or experience of God.

1. Concerning the view of God as the source of love, Yunus does not erase an image of a transcendent and monotheistic God. Yet, Yunus speaks out for "*dignitas hominis*" or an image of human beings not as an outcast, but as an extension of God's reality and love. Unlike the dogma, he shares his insight that humans are not only God's creation but also God's reflection. Compared to Yunus, Jacopone's view is more dualistic by rejecting the world and human essence. His satire and rage seemed to point out human sinfulness, including the arrogance of some Franciscans at his time.
2. Yunus might enter intimacy with God through love, but he seemed to emphasize God's unspoken mystery. He is more an apophatic rather than a cataphatic mystic. For the cataphatic, God is believed as the One who revealed the Divine plan, characters, or essence to human beings. (Fan 2018) Therefore, different from Yunus, Jacopone could cling to the personified or anthropomorphic God that his faith had taught him. In each stage of his journey through inner pain, enlightenment, and union, he could relate each of the experiences to the suffering, death, and resurrection or victory of Christ.

3. Last but most important for Jacopone, God's love is beyond human's understanding as God incarnated in Christ wishes to sacrifice and endures pains in manifesting the Divine Love for human sake. Furthermore, as love is the essence of God's nature, Jacopone views God incarnated to manifest the Almighty's love in Jesus Christ. Thus, Jacopone's relationship with Jesus is like a lover and a Beloved. Christ was not a symbol, but the reality that Jacopone falls in love and senses His deep pains in the process of redeeming human beings or bringing humans to a love relationship with God. (Rassekh 1987, 12).

The relevance and contribution of the study are as follow. First, the study points out the richness of forms that might convey the depth of spiritual life of people from different religious or social, and cultural contexts. The fact can expand many believers' perspectives of spirituality or challenge people to delve deeper into the essence of their core spiritual life. Second, if the tumultuous uncertainties in 13th century Turkey and Italy are similar to the present dynamics of many nations, the poetic expressions of spiritual insight might serve many people today more effectively as they might be struggling with a spiritual yearning that many current religious symbols, expressions, and forms might need creative modification to fulfil it. Third, if many Christians view that the Muslims centre more on laws and doctrines in their religion, such a view can be modified with the proof that in Islam, in the core teaching of the Islamic faith, love also has a central position.

The richness of the poems of Yunus Emre and Lauds of Jacopone da Todi might need further study. One of the questions that might need an answer is related to differences in the meaning of human self-hood in their view, the spiritual journey stages, and the meaning of death as the concepts that appear several times in Yunus Emre's works and Jacopone da Todi's Lauds.

Reference

Başgöz, İlhan. 2020. Yunus Emre, Vol 2. Istanbul, Turkey: Pan Yayincilik.

Başkal, Zekeriya. 2010. Yunus Emre, The Sufi Poet in Love. Clifton, New Jersey: Blue Dome Press. https://bluedomepress.com/product/yunus-emre-the-sufi-poet-in-love/.

Bombaci, Allessio. 1956. *Storia Della Letteratura Turca Dall'Antico Impero Di Mongolia All'Odierna Turchia.* 1st ed. Milano: Nuova accademia editrice.

Casella, Mario. 1920. "Iacopone Da Todi." *Archivum Romanioum* 4: 231–339, 429–85.

D'Ancona, Alessandro. 1914. *Iacopone Da Todi Il Giullare Di Dio Del Secolo XIII.* Todi: Casa ed. Atanor.

Dilaver, Faruk. 2021. *Yunus Emre: His Life, Perspective, and Poems.* Ankara, Turkey: Dilaver Yayincilik.

Faiz, Sufa (trans). 1992. *The City Of The Heart: Yunus Emre's Verses of Wisdom and Love.* Rockport, MA: Elements Inc. https://id.scribd.com/document/425617667/The-City-of-the-Heart-Yunus-Emres-Verses-of-Love.

Fan, Jiani. 2018. "Images of Mind, Images of God: Mirror as Metaphor in Chinese Buddhism and Early Mysticism." *Buddhist-Christian Studies.* https://doi.org/10.1353/BCS.2018.0017.

Franca ed, Ageno. 1953. *Jacopone Da Todi: Laudi Di Trattato e Detti.* Florence, Italy: Le Monnier.

Franceschini, Marta Irene. 2012. "'Mysticism, Love and Poetry' A Comparative Study of Amir Khusrau and Jacopone Da Todi." Jawaharlal Nehru University. chrome-extension://efaidnbmnnnibpcajpcglclefindmkaj/viewer.html?pdfurl=http%3A%2F%2Fmeykhane.altervista.org%2FFRANCESCHINITesi.pdf&clen=665901&chunk=true.

Gölpınarlı, Abdülbâkî, Ed. 1943. *Yunus Emre Divani.* Istanbul, Turkey: A. Halit Kitabevi.

Gölpınarlı, Abdülbaki. 1961. *Yunus Emre ve Tasavvuf.* Istanbul, Turkey: Remzi Kitabevi.

Greenberg, Yudit Kornberg. 2016. "Erotic Representations of the Divine." In *Oxford Research Encyclopedia of Religion.* Oxford University Press https://doi.org/10.1093/ACREFORE/9780199340378.013.120.

Hughes, Serge, and Elizabeth Hughes. 1982. *Jacopone Da Todi: The Lauds.* Edited by Richard. Ed. Payne. Ramsey, NJ: Paulist Press.

"Jacopone Da Todi." n.d. *The Canterbury Dictionary of Hymnology*. https://hymnology.hymnsam.co.uk/j/jacopone-da-todi.

Köprülü, Mehmet Fuat, Gary Leiser, and Robert. Dankoff. 2006. *Early Mystics in Turkish Literature*. Routledge Taylor & Francis Group. London, UK: Routledge.

Küçük, Demet, and Havva Aslan. 2008. *Selected Poems of The Divan of Yunus Emre*. 1st ed. Istanbul, Turkey: Profil Yayincilik. Kindle Edition.

Mancini, Franco. 2006. *Le Laude: Iacopone Da Todi, Mancini, F.* Roma-Bari, Italy: Laterza. https://www.amazon.it/laude-Iacopone-Todi/dp/8842079707.

Meerssemann, Giles Gerard. 1962. "Disciplinati e Penitenti n El Duecento, Il Movimento Dei Disciplinati Nel Settimo Centenario Dal Suo Inizio (Perugia. 1260)." Perugia.

Nagatomo, Shigenori. 2000. "The Logic of the Diamond Sutra: A Is Not A, Therefore It Is A." *Asian Philosophy* 10 (3): 213–44. https://doi.org/10.1080/09552360020011277.

Novati, Francesco. 1908. *Freschi e Minii Del Dugento: Conferenze e Letture*. Milano: Casa Editrice L.F. Cogliati. https://archive.org/stream/FreschiEMiniiDelDugento/Freschi_e_minii_del_dugento_djvu.txt.

Plouvier, P. 2002. *Poesia e Mistica (Poetry and Mysticism)*. Vatican: Libreria Editrice Vaticana. https://www.libreriauniversitaria.it/poesia-mistica-plouvier-paule-libreria/libro/9788820973322.

Rassekh, Chohre. 1987. "Mystical Poetry of Jalaluddin Rumi and Jacopone Da Todi: A Comparison." The University of British Columbia.

Sanctis, Francesco De. 1961. *Storia Della Letteratura Italiana. Opere*. Ed. Niccolo Gallo. Milano-Napol: Ricciardi.

Sezer, Ahmed Rusen. 1967. "The Concept of Love in Yunus Emre's Thought." McGill University.

Tatçi, Mustafa. 1990. *Yunus Emre Divani*. Ankara: Kultur bakanligi.

———. 2012. *Yunus Emre Divanı*. Istambul: Diyanet İşleri Başkanlığı. https://www.kitapyurdu.com/kitap/yunus-emre-divani/528420.html.

"Troubadour." 2021. *Merriam-Webster*. 2021. https://www.merriam-webster.com/dictionary/troubadour.

Underhill, Evelyn. 1919. *Jacopone Da Todi, Poet and Mystic 1228-1306, A Spiritual Biography*. London and Toronto: JM Dents and Sons Ltd.

Wallace, John R. 2019. *Interpreting Love Narratives in East Asian Literature and Film: : The Status of Traditional Worldviews and Values*. MountainView, California: Berkeleypressbook.pub.

Zardin, Danilo. n.d. "'Christ Draws Me Totally:' Jacopone and the Paradox of Total Love." Ilsussidiario.Net. Accessed October 14, 2021. https://www.olschki.it.

Epilogue

This work begins with the realisation that despite the technological development which allows humans to master time and space, there are many dimensions in their inner or spiritual journey that have not been deeply recognized.

The role of a turning point in humans' life, the destination of a meaningful life journey, and the union with the Divine are a few of the spiritual insights that might further exploration. Indeed, the spiritual journey that each person needs contains a price to pay: learning and changing. Both mean that each stage demands the Homo Viator to leave something and obtain something new.

The horizon is extremely wide. As many spiritual masters recognize, human words are limited to describe it, but the journey does have stages and a path to be found. No other way to experience progress if the travellers do not wish to embrace humility and trust in the Divine's love,

Contents

Introduction	5
An Implicit Good News in a Javanese indigenous religious poem	7
Homo Viator: Comparative Study of Serat Jatimurti with the Parable of the Prodigal Son	29
The Meaning of Love in Yunus Emre and Jacopone da Todi's Works	53
Epilogue	88

www.ingramcontent.com/pod-product-compliance
Lightning Source LLC
Chambersburg PA
CBHW070939240426
43667CB00036B/2433